Le Pain Quotidien

cook + book
memories and recipes

Alain Coumont
Jean-Pierre Gabriel – text and photography

FRANÇOISE BLOUARD

My heartfelt thanks to Simone Lacroix, Madeleine Limet and Marguerite Begon, to Jacqueline Begon, my mother, to Pierre Coumont, my father, and to everyone with a passionate interest in good but simple food who inspired and supported me and who sometimes sowed seeds of doubt in my mind, thus enabling me to forge ahead and try to fulfil my vocation as an inveterate proponent of 'real food'.

Alain Coumont

And, from the bottom of my heart, thanks to all who, day by day, make the daily bread what it is.

Text and photography *Jean-Pierre Gabriel*

Recipes *Alain Coumont*

Graphic design and typesetting *Oeyen en Winters*

Translation *Laura Macilwaine*

Colour separation and printing *Snoeck-Ducaju, Ghent (Belgium)*

Final editing *Florence Kévers, Louella Salvador & Philippe Le Roux*

© 2005 Editions Françoise Blouard, Jean-Pierre Gabriel and Alain Coumont

D/2005/10.612/3

ISBN 2-9600487-3-3

www.francoiseblouard.com

www.lepainquotidien.com

cook + book

Flour, water and salt

The story of Le Pain Quotidien began at precisely 7 am on October 26 1990, when the first Le Pain Quotidien store, located at 16 rue Dansaert, opened its doors and its very first customers crossed the threshold.

No one, especially not baker Alain Coumont, could possibly have imagined on that first day that things would develop very much further than a trendy bakery in a district of Brussels considered fashionable at the time, namely the area around the Stock Exchange.

The adventure had started a year or two earlier when Alain Coumont, an up-and-coming young chef, decided to make his own bread because he remembered Poilâne bread, for which he had acquired a taste while working in Paris. It took shape when, bouncing ideas around and taking advantage of all opportunities which happened to come his way and on which he could capitalize, he put the finishing touches to his store, so that its look was exactly what he wanted.

In October 1990, Alain Coumont had left nothing to chance. Down town, he was no longer to be seen wearing his chef's whites. Instead, he now wore a slightly spotted clerical grey apron, the kind which cashiers in old-fashioned hardware stores used to wear in the past. He had chosen the outfit which went with his occupation and used it as a form of advertising. For whatever reason, he had innate marketing skills and he knew exactly how to tap into them.

In reality, the story of Le Pain Quotidien had started long before, with a small child wandering around his grandmother's kitchens, opposite Huy train station, and standing on a chair, making his very first pastries in the home of a distant aunt, the person who introduced him to cooking and baking. It became rooted in his everyday habits and convictions when, as a student, he used organic flour to bake bread at home on Sundays to take with him to school.

Somewhere in his memory everything was already embedded, everything which contributed to the development of his project. This started out as an idea in the mind of a man who simply wanted to bake good bread with flour, water and salt. But this story, which at the outset was merely a personal venture, materialized into a business designed to appeal to a niche market and to make a profit, immediately set a trend. It transcended simply satisfying customer demand.

Le Pain Quotidien was such a strong and robust concept that it was born to become autonomous, to break free at the earliest opportunity from its founding father. The people who come to buy their bread, to sit at a large communal table next to people whom they do not know, eating bread and jam and drinking coffee, consider themselves to be its legatees, seeing it as a legacy bequeathed to them.

Like so many other adventures, Le Pain Quotidien has had its ups and downs. Alain Coumont is part of this story, which is still as Belgian as ever, if not more so, just as it was right at the very beginning. We decided to select a number of extracts and tell them in the form of nine stories that sparked particularly vivid memories of the adventure which started all those years ago.

I met Alain, intrigued by a letter which he had sent me, probably the same photocopied missive which other journalists had received at the same time. He described a career path studded with prestigious names, including Guérard, Robuchon, Blanc and Senderens, and announced the forthcoming opening of his restaurant, Le Café du Dôme. At the same time, the press attaché of Robert Laffont, the French publishing house, drew my attention to a young Belgian chef, who was about to publish a book co-authored by Michel Guérard.

Even then, Alain Coumont emerged as a man in a class of his own and nothing has changed. He is a loyal friend and that is no doubt why I am putting the finishing touches to this manuscript, which has rekindled the memory of so many seemingly insignificant moments, of breakfast time eating bread and drinking coffee on grandma's oilcloth-covered kitchen table. Childhood for ever...

Jean-Pierre Gabriel, Brussels, September 21 2005

A 'sweet-toothed', hunky-dory childhood

I was born in Huy, a small town on the river Meuse in southern Belgium. My parents had a grocery store in the town, on the corner of rue des Fouarges and rue des Rôtisseurs. My father had trained as a chef at the hotel management school in Namur. But as my grandfather had fallen ill, he had been forced to give up on the idea of pursuing any personal plans that he might have had and to take over the family business and support his mother instead.

The life story of my grandfather, Fernand Coumont, is quite extraordinary and reflects an entire era in itself.

François, my great grandfather, was a manservant in a country house in the region. He had been given a small plot of land as a kitchen garden, on which he grew vegetables. When he was nine or ten years old, my grandfather used to walk to the market in Huy, the nearest town, with a cart drawn by a dog. Together they made a 30-kilometre round trip to sell the vegetables grown in the kitchen garden at Huy market. When my grandfather grew up he became more professional. He met Madeleine, my grandmother, and bought a small store in Huy. It was his first grocery and he was what used to be known as a costermonger, a sort of street merchant. He had a cart, horse-drawn this time, and went round farms. He collected butter and cheeses, poultry and game, eggs, potatoes, honey, fruit – anything in fact which he could sell in town.

A little later, one of his cousins, an industrialist from Brussels by the name of Lallemand, bought a fine property, a former bank, in Huy, and rented it cheaply to my grandfather. We lived in the apartment above the grocery store. So it could be said that I was born with a silver spoon in my mouth.

I remember the cellar. It had been the strong room. When the bankers left, the safes had been removed and the gaping alcoves had been turned into storage areas for cans. Each alcove had its speciality: litre-size cans of peaches next to half-litre cans, canned tomatoes, concentrates, etc.

As far as his father's business sense is concerned, my father recounts an amusing anecdote. It happened during World War Two, when the German occupiers were printing paper money to pay their soldiers. I have never known how or why my grandfather smelt a rat and realized that once the war was over this paper money would be worth much less. But he asked his customers to pay for their eggs, lettuces, etc., in coins only!

As the currency was indeed devalued, paper money was replaced, but not coins. It would have been far too expensive for the country. I believe it took my grandfather ten years to dispose of all the coins which he had accumulated. All his suppliers were paid in coins. Every evening, the family went down to the cellar to fetch a bucket of coins, then used newspaper to make 'twists' for 5 centime, 10 centime, 20 centime coins. My father and my uncle tell how when they were kids, there were heaps of coins piled high and how they used to amuse themselves by jumping into them, like sand dunes.

My father took over the family business in the 1960s. The Golden Sixties. He went upmarket, raising the quality standard and extending the range. Twice a week, he drove an ancient red Chevrolet truck to Brussels, to buy vegetables at the early morning market. His gods were the buyers for Rob, the luxury grocery store in Brussels. They had large baskets inscribed with 'Rob' in gold lettering. They were the lords of the early morning market. The finest and most expensive produce was for them. That made a big impression on my father. When he took over the family business, he used Coumont 'the fresh produce specialist' as a slogan, copying it from Rob. Nowadays, people copy slogans from London or Milan. At the time, Brussels was almost like a foreign country. My father really did raise standards; he started selling foie gras, small packs of caviar and truffle peel and installed a fish tank with live lobsters in the store. That's the background.

Women first got me interested in cooking. Marguerite Begon, my maternal grandmother, was a cook. She and René, my grandfather, kept a hotel and restaurant opposite the north station in Huy, as was often the case in medium-sized towns at the time. Unsurprisingly, it was called Hôtel du Nord. The café-restaurant was called Le Cap Nord. I can still see my grandmother in her kitchen. To me, as a child, it seemed huge. And in fact, probably was.

There were six Nestor Martin gas stoves in a row, fuelled by 4-burner gas cylinders, so there were a total of 24 gas burners. She also used Tefal frying pans – domestic rather than truly professional kitchen utensils. She was a workaholic. My grandparents never went abroad, in fact I don't think that they ever even ventured as far as the North Sea coast in Belgium. With the train station opposite their house and in a country as small as Belgium, it seems incredible. But that's how it was.

It's somewhat paradoxical but it was not really with her that I learned to cook. There was also my paternal grandmother and, even more importantly as things turned out, Aunt Simone. We called her aunt but she was in fact the mother-in-law of my uncle, my father's brother. She lived in the country with her husband, who was the station master of Moha, a tiny village in the region.

They grew potatoes and kept poultry and rabbits. She made her jams with fruit from the garden, went to the farm to collect her milk every morning. I remember that she boiled it before putting it in the refrigerator.

Every Saturday she baked 12 to 15 tarts. And every Sunday, the entire family came to drink bowls of coffee and eat rice tart, gooseberry tart and pound cake waffles!

She also did a lot of home-preserving, using Weck canning jars. There were preserved beans, tomatoes, plums, cherries and the like. So it was really with Aunt Simone that I learned to cook. When I was two or three years old, she used to stand me on a chair while she was making her pastry. It was pâte levée sucrée (sweet bread dough) that she rolled out. She put it on round baking tins and snipped the edges off with her rolling pin. I used to make little apple turnovers with these scraps of dough.

That was why sweet things appealed to me, like any child who likes sweets and candies.

After this fruit tart phase, when I was six or seven years old I started to read. There were only two cook books at home. The first book was of the domestic, rudimentary kind, a free gift with the purchase of a pressure cooker. The second was one my father received from the hotel management school when he was awarded a prize as the best dining room student. It was a thick cook book published by Flammarion and entitled "L'Encyclopédie de la Gastronomie française" (Encyclopaedia of French Gastronomy).

All the recipes were illustrated with photos, but everything was classic, with poached mayonnaise, mimosa eggs, served on long oval dishes called torpedo dishes! I taught myself to cook with this book, reading recipes and hints. I started by making chocolate mousse, cream puffs and éclairs. I had a sweet tooth until I was 13 or 14, as far as I can remember. Before that age I was never tempted by anything savoury.

From flour to sourdough starter bread

Bread forms part of the family of living and evolving foodstuffs whose special flavour, personality and individuality appeal to us. For bread is a product of fermentation, like cheese, yogurts and kefirs, beer, wine and cider, to name but a few. Fermentation is dependent on the action of micro-organisms, living things which convert the sugars contained in the raw materials, generating in the process a whole range of aromas and flavours characterizing a finished product, expressing its "terroir"; its place of origin in the broadest sense, in a word, giving it its unique personality.

There is naturally a great temptation to channel, standardize and dominate this process and thus to create uniformity.

Wine and its vinification provide a telling example of the difference which can exist between total control, industrialization of fermentation and making good use of the yeasts found naturally on the surface of grapes.

Roughly the same rules apply to bread and bread-making and the same trends are apparent. Baker's yeast, an industrial product, has largely superseded the sourdough variety, a change which occurred on a massive scale during the twentieth century.

Things were quite different for thousands of years, since the day when a small piece of dough which a baker had forgotten about produced a different kind of bread. The dough, which had been left in the open air, had swollen, becoming more elastic and spongy.

It has since been learned that this change in texture is the culmination of a process involving two successive stages. During the first stage, an enzyme called amylase converts the

Larousse gastronomique says that in baking, the concept refers to 'sour dough', used to leaven bread.. Every day the baker has to 'refresh' his "levain" (sourdough), by kneading it with flour and water. He uses part of it that day and keeps the other half, the "chef" (dough-like starter) to repeat the same operation the next day.

starch in the flour into maltose, a sugar consisting of two linked glucose units.

As they now have food available, the agents responsible for fermentation can get to work and convert the sugar into alcohol (ethanol) and carbon dioxide. The bubbles given off by the carbon dioxide cause the dough to swell and consequently create the cavities which make its texture lighter and spongy.

Without wishing to describe the whole of the living process of bread-making, one of the main players, the keystone, so to speak, of the process which gives the dough its plasticity, needs to be mentioned here. It is a substance which the Chinese very accurately describe as the 'muscle of flour', namely gluten.

It is thanks to the action of the gluten proteins – combined with the water incorporated into the dough – that the dough has a degree of elasticity, which allows pressure to be put on the lump of dough to flatten it, after which it gradually returns to its original shape.

In terms of pure physics, the gluten weaves a network of proteins which give dough its expansion capacity, through the action of carbon dioxide bubbles.

These purely technical phenomena occur in roughly the same way, whether baker's yeast or sourdough starter is used.

If one is interested in the flavour of things, in sensations appealing to the taste buds, in food which is eye-catching and smells delicious, making life more pleasurable and love of eating a virtue, in short, if one is interested in the soul and essence of food, then one should take the time to nurture sourdough starter, as

From flour to sourdough starter bread

According to The Oxford Companion to Food., there are three stages in the creation of a "levain" (sourdough). First, a basic mix is prepared. In its simplest form it is a dough made from flour and water, providing food and moisture for the "yeast" spores which the baker hopes are present. When this mixture is fermented, part is used to make a bake of bread rise.

The success of sourdough starter is also dependent on regularity. From the first to the last day, morning and evening, the starter dough comes into contact again with the flour, water and salt, to 'refresh' it, leading to a sort of permanent rejuvenation.

All the ingredients of the sourdough starter are used at 'room temperature', the optimum temperature at which the starter dough will rise is 27-28°C.

Steven L. Kaplan so aptly puts it. To paraphrase his description, sourdough starter is made from wild yeasts and bacteria present in the raw materials or the ambient air of the bake house. It is perpetuated by systematic successive 'refreshment' (or enrichment), ensuring selection and reproduction of the flora, consisting primarily of a combination of its acidifying bacteria and its own yeasts. Dough made using a sourdough starter produces bread whose cream-coloured texture is considerably denser, more irregular, supple and elastic than bread made using baker's yeast. Its crust is thicker. It keeps better naturally. It prides itself on being more nutritious because it is richer in vitamins and certain enzymes.

However, making good bread without the right type of flour is an impossibility. Whether used to make sourdough starter or bread – wheat or rye – the flour used by Le Pain Ouotidien is always stone-ground. Stones grind the flour more finely than metal cylinders, the corollary being that the bran particles are smaller in size. The presence of bran particles means that bread made with stone-ground flour has a more pronounced flavour, evocative of crunchy whole cereal grains.

By the same token, the germ is also more atomized, making its separation from the ground cereal more difficult. With its high oil content (these oils also being essential to the proper rising of the bread), the germ enhances the flour's nutritional value. The downside is that these fatty substances ultimately cause the flour to go off more quickly. Stone-ground flour's shelf-life is therefore limited to a few months.

Le Pain Quotidien's sourdough starter

TO PRODUCE A SOURDOUGH STARTER, THE FOLLOWING ARE REQUIRED :

A TOTAL OF 2KG OF STONE-GROUND WHOLE WHEAT FLOUR, 1.2 LITRES OF SPRING WATER AND GREY (I.E. UNREFINED) SALT.

The creation of a sourdough starter is an investment where patience is key. Starting from wheat flour, water and salt – the ingredients in the sourdough bread baked by Le Pain Quotidien – a fermentation process is set in motion, reaching its climax on the eleventh day.

- THE FIRST DAY

In the morning: in an earthenware or stainless steel bowl, quickly mix by hand 100g of flour, 60g of spring water and a pinch of salt. Cover with a plate and leave at kitchen temperature.

In the evening: 12 hours later, add 100g of flour, 60g of water and a pinch of salt, then mix quickly and cover with a plate.

- THE SECOND DAY

In the morning: keep only 150g of dough and add to it 100g of flour and 60g of water, mix quickly, cover and keep at room temperature.

In the evening: 12 hours later, keep only 150g of dough and add 100g of flour, 60g of water and a pinch of salt, then mix quickly and cover with a plate.

- FROM THE THIRD TO THE TENTH DAY

In the morning and the evening, repeat the second day's operations. On the morning of the eleventh day, start on the last stage.

- THE ELEVENTH DAY

In the morning the bread is kneaded for the first time.

Take all the sourdough starter (310g) and add 500g of flour, 300g of water and a pinch of salt. Mix and leave to rest for 5 hours.

It takes 5 hours for the dough to acquire the status of ready-to-use sourdough starter. By that point its total weight has increased to 1110g.

Sourdough wheat bread

MAKES TWO 2KG ROUND LOAVES (WEIGHT AFTER BAKING) :

720G SOURDOUGH STARTER, 2.5KG STONE-GROUND FLOUR (TYPE 85),
1.75 LITRES FILTERED WATER OR SPRING WATER, 40G UNREFINED SEA SALT.

An oven with a stone hearth is essential for this type of bread. If you do not have one in your oven, look for a 4-5cm thick heat-resistant slab of stone, which may be lava stone, refractory brick, granite and similar stones. The use of steam is fundamental in the crust formation process, which conditions the texture of the inside of the loaf. In a dry atmosphere, the crust quickly solidifies, becomes airtight and prevents the gases from escaping. But these gases are what contribute to the formation of cavities in the bread, guaranteeing its elasticity and relative lightness.

- Ensure that all the ingredients are at a temperature of 25°-27°C. Put them all in the food processor bowl and, using the dough hook, knead at low speed for 3 minutes, then at high speed for 2 minutes and finally at slow speed for 5 minutes. Leave to rest in the bowl at a temperature of 27°-28°C for an hour and a half.
- Stir and compress the dough every 15 minutes by whizzing the hook for 3 seconds. This operation is therefore carried out six times, giving more body to the dough.
- To make two 2kg loaves, separate the dough into two 2.3kg lumps. Place them on a floured worktop (counter). This is when the process proper of making the bread begins. First of all, the lumps of dough need to be flattened to a thickness of 7-8cm, by literally 'boxing' the centre. Then stretch the dough to its four corners (think of the four cardinal points of a compass), then fold back each point to the centre of the lump.
- Repeat the operation at the four intermediate points (which would be the north east, south east, south west and north west here). Press firmly with the palm of the hand or the fist in the centre, to ensure that the eight points are sealed. Pick up the lump of dough and turn it over (top to bottom and vice versa), then put it into a well floured linen-lined bread basket.

- Cover with a clean cloth and leave to rest at a temperature ranging between 26°C and 28°C. Leave to 'prove' for between 3 1/2 and 4 1/2 hours depending on fermentation activity and the desired degree of acidity. The longer the dough is left to rest, the greater the acidity.
- Meanwhile, wrap up the remaining dough in a plastic bag and refrigerate for a few days, until the next bread-baking session.
- Just before baking, turn the dough in the bread basket out onto the stone hearth of an oven which has been preheated to a temperature of 240°C.
- Using a razor blade, make one or more criss-cross marks on the surface of the lump of dough, thus adding the 'baker's signature'.
- At this point, ensure that there is a source of steam, either by placing a small dish of hot water at the bottom of the oven or by spraying the surface of the bread and the burning stone, using a spray bottle, just before closing the oven again.
- Bake the bread for around an hour and ten minutes, to obtain a loaf weighing 2kg.
- Leave to rest for a few hours at least before slicing. Sourdough bread of this kind takes 2-3 days to mature properly, depending on the season and the atmosphere.

The small 200g lump which has been refrigerated will be the starter for the sourdough culture which may be made several days later. To do so, take this piece of dough out of the refrigerator. Return it to room temperature under a clean cloth, then add 330g of flour and 2dl of water. Mix and wait for 5 hours to produce the starter which will enable two further 2kg loaves (or four 1kg loaves) to be made.

Roasted hazelnut and raisin flûte

MAKES 12 FLÛTES (SMALL AND THIN FRENCH STICKS):

720G SOURDOUGH WHEAT BREAD DOUGH, 360G RAISINS (SMYRNA VARIETY), 360G WHOLE HAZELNUTS, 50G WATER, 1G DRIED OR 3 G FRESH BAKER'S YEAST, 1 TSP SALT.

For this type of bread, as for the baguette à l'ancienne, use of sourdough starter is more a question of adding taste than of raising the dough. Its combination with baker's yeast does, however, enable the proportion of sourdough starter required to be reduced. If sourdough starter alone is used to raise such small amounts of dough, the time needed for the fermentation process to be completed will be longer than with baker's yeast, leading the surface of the lumps of dough to dry out.

- Ensure that all the ingredients are at the room temperature of the kitchen.
- Arrange the hazelnuts in a single layer in a hot non-stick frying pan and roast them for a few minutes. Transfer to a dish and leave to cool.
- Preheat the oven to its maximum temperature. Put the ingredients into a large bowl and knead with both hands, so that everything is thoroughly mixed together. Divide into 120g lumps of dough.
- Place them on a floured worktop (counter) and using floured fingers, form into cylinder shapes measuring approximately 25cm in length.
- Leave to prove (rise) for 1 1/2 hours covered with a sheet of plastic wrap at room temperature (26-28°C).
- Bake in a very hot oven preheated to 250°C for 15-20 minutes until they have turned a nice golden colour. (Place a small dish with 1 cup of boiling water on the bottom of the oven to generate steam).

Baguette à l'ancienne (old-fashioned style)

FOR THE SOURDOUGH:

100G FLOUR (TYPE 65), 65G WATER, 1G SALT, 2G FRESH BAKER'S YEAST.

FOR THE DOUGH: 165G SOURDOUGH, 1KG FLOUR (TYPE 65), 650G WATER, 18G SALT, 10G FRESH BAKER'S YEAST OR 3 G OF ACTIVE DRY YEAST.

ON THE FIRST DAY: prepare a sourdough with the baker's yeast.
- Quickly mix these ingredients, put in a bowl covered with a clean cloth, then leave at kitchen temperature for a minimum of 12 hours.
  ON THE SECOND DAY: Put the water, the yeast, the sourdough and the flour into the food processor bowl and blend at slow speed with the dough hook for 1 minute.
- Add the salt, knead at medium speed for 3 minutes, turn off.
  Scrape the sides of the bowl with a plastic spatula to remove any lumps and knead at low speed for a further 4 minutes.
- Leave the dough to rest in the bowl for an hour and twenty minutes, whizzing the hook for 3 seconds every 20 minutes, or 4 times during resting time. The purpose is to stir and compress the dough, to give it more body.
- Take the dough out of the bowl and put it on a lightly floured worktop (counter).
- Cut into four 450g lumps, quickly roll them in the flour and leave to rest for 5 minutes.
- Carefully stretch the lumps of dough lengthwise, with hands and the working surface still floured, to produce 40cm long 'baguettes'. This involves pressing the sides while rolling and making to-and-fro movements.
- Place the shaped lumps of dough on a large clean cloth, also floured. Fold the cloth between each baguette, so that they do not touch one another. Cover with a plastic sheet (not food film) and leave to 'prove' for approximately 25-35 minutes, depending on room temperature. The hotter it is, the more quickly the bread will rise, and vice versa.
- Preheat the oven and the baking tray (place a small dish with 1 cup of boiling water on the bottom of the oven to generate steam).
- Carefully place the lumps of dough on a floured baking tray, one at a time. The tray must be thin and the size of the lumps of dough. Using a razor blade, make 5 incisions, obliquely and slantwise. The blade must be at an angle. Place in the oven on the baking stone.
- Bake at 240°C for approximately 20 minutes, until the bread has turned a nice colour.

Given the size of domestic ovens, make half-baguettes (225g lumps of dough) in the same way.

This dough is also suitable for regular bread baked in rectangular metal tins (pans). 'Proving' time will be longer (approximately 45 minutes).

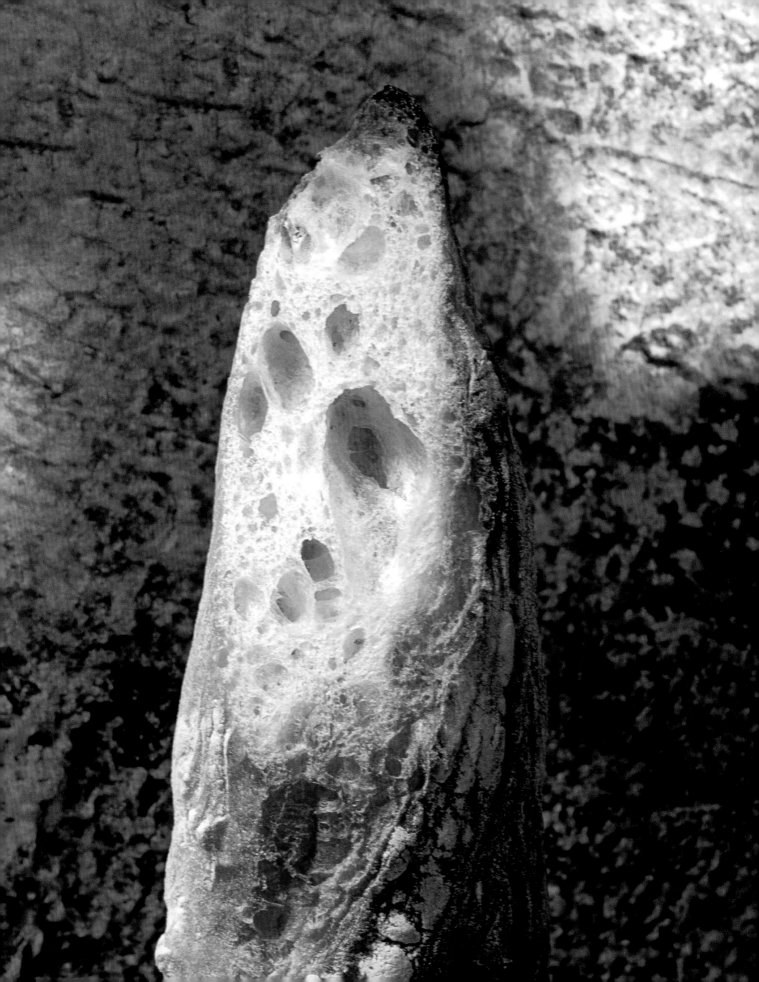

Ten-seed whole cereal bread

MAKES 2 LOAVES:

100G PEARL BARLEY, 100G MILLET, 100G QUINOA, 100G OAT GRAINS OR FLAKES, 100G KAMUT, 100G BUCKWHEAT, 100G ROUND RICE FROM THE CAMARGUE, 100G RYE FLOUR, 50G SUNFLOWER SEEDS, 25G SESAME SEEDS, 25G LINSEEDS, 15G GUÉRANDE GREY SALT, 75G DRIED SOURDOUGH STARTER OR 200G FRESH SOURDOUGH STARTER, 1 LITRE WATER, 1 TBSP VIRGIN SUNFLOWER OIL (TO GREASE THE MOULDS).

- Weigh the 7 cereals and mix them in a large bowl. Remove 300g and crush finely in a vegetable mill or food processor.
- Mix the crushed cereals with the rye flour, the salt and the linseeds, sunflower and sesame seeds. Set aside.
- Moisten the remaining 500g of cereals with the litre of water (20°C) and leave to soak at room temperature for 48 hours.
- Two days later, drain to remove the soaking water which has not been absorbed. Pour on the crushed cereals, add the powdered sourdough starter and mix thoroughly. Add the soaked cereals.
- Preheat the oven to 250°C.
- Mix the contents of the bowl and transfer to two non-stick lightly greased rectangular moulds. Cover the upper surface of each lump of dough with a rectangle of lightly greased baking paper.
- Bake at 250°C for 20 minutes, reduce the temperature to 150°C and bake for a further 30 minutes. Leave to cool in the moulds for 3 hours.
- Turn out of the moulds and wrap the loaves in food film or put them in a Tupperware container. Store in a cool place for at least 24 hours before eating.
- Slice thinly with a sharp, smooth-bladed knife which has been lightly greased beforehand.

Small individual loaves can also be made, by weighing out 80-100g 'lumps' of dough. In that case, baking time is shortened to 25 minutes (at 250°C). Store them in a cool place.

Whole cereal bread can be eaten as it is or toasted when taken out of the refrigerator. It is absolutely delicious spread with butter and sea salt.

Gluten-free whole cereal petits lingots (lingot-shaped mini-loaves)

FOR 20 MINI-LOAVES:

200G WHOLE MILLET, 200G QUINOA, 200G BUCKWHEAT, 200G ROUND RICE FROM THE CAMARGUE, 50G SUNFLOWER SEEDS, 50G SESAME SEEDS, 50G LINSEEDS, 50G PUMPKIN SEEDS, 20 G SODIUM BICARBONATE ALSO CALLED BAKING SODA, 1 LITRE SPRING WATER, 10G GUÉRANDE GREY SALT, 1 TBSP VIRGIN SUNFLOWER OIL (TO GREASE THE MOULDS)

Like all bread, these petits lingots, can be frozen. They can be removed from the freezer and easily brought back to the right temperature if they are toasted twice.

A large loaf can also be baked. To do so, follow the baking instructions in the recipe for whole cereal bread (previous pages).

Another less common gluten-free 'cereal' is amaranth, a plant typically grown in Latin America. It can be used to supplement the mix of cereals in this recipe.

- Two days ahead, mix together the four gluten-free cereals in a large bowl. Take 300g of this mixture and grind it finely in a vegetable mill or food processor bowl.
- Mix the ground cereals with the salt and the oilseeds (linseed, sunflower, sesame and pumpkin seeds). Set aside.
- Moisten the remaining 500g of cereals with the litre of water (temperature: 20°C). Leave to soak at room temperature for 36-48 hours.
- Two days later, heat the oven up to 250°C.
- Drain off the juice which has not been absorbed by the cereals left to soak and pour it over the ground cereals. Add the baking soda and mix thoroughly.
- Add the soaked cereals. Mix well and fill lightly greased non-stick individual rectangular moulds.
- Bake in the oven at 250°C for 20-25 minutes. Leave to cool in the moulds for an hour.
- Remove from the moulds and eat the same day. Just before serving, toast the petits lingots so that they are warm and crispy.
- They may also be served with good quality slightly salted butter or a small dish of virgin colza or sunflower oil.

Apprenticeship

The turning point came in the USA. I was 15 and was spending the school holidays there as part of an exchange programme organized by a Belgo-American friendship association. My parents had had an American student as a house guest the previous year so they could send one of their children over to the USA the following year. It happened to be me.

I arrived at the McDonough family's home in East Greenwich near Newport, Rhode Island in July 1976, the year of the USA's bicentenary. It was not very far from Boston or Cape Cod. They took me to Niagara Falls and to Washington DC. We went on a short trip to New York.

Then one day, while I was watching ABC on television in my room, I happened to see a long feature on Michel Guérard in Eugénie-les-Bains. He had been named 'Man of the Year' by Time Magazine. His photo was on the cover, with the title 'Hold the Butter'. His book , entitled "La grande cuisine minceur", had been translated into English for the North American market under the title 'The Cuisine of Slimness' and had been a phenomenal success, becoming a bestseller. I was bowled over. When I had seen my grandparents working night and day, I had certainly not been attracted by their occupation. But this was something else – a totally different ball game.

When I returned home to Belgium, I said to my father: "I want to go to hotel management school". We went to Namur, but as it was already September 1 it was too late to enrol, so I had to wait a year. When I finally started, it was really funny because all the old teachers remembered my father.

That was the time when the adventure started. The first book I bought in 1978, at the beginning of my first year, was "La Cuisine gourmande" by Michel Guérard, which had just been published in France by Robert Laffont. That is where I discovered the world of savoury food.

I spent four years at the hotel management school in Namur. When

I turned 18 and had learned to drive, I started to cook for people at weekends. My parents had organized a takeaway department in their store but there was no catering service as such for private receptions. As customers often asked about home catering, my father told them that his son was a student at a hotel management school and could come and do the catering for them. So I started to cook meals for 12 in the homes of the town's dignitaries.

During the week I lodged in Namur. On Friday afternoons, I left the school at around 3 or 4 pm and got home at around 5.30 pm. I quite often had a meal scheduled for the evening. My father had prepared the order according to the menu. I went to people's homes and prepared everything in their kitchen, nothing having been set up in advance. I peeled vegetables, boned young pigeons and dissected pigs' trotters. It was always stressful. I generally took a pal from school with me, to wait on table. That's how we started, first in Huy, providing a catering service for two or three families. Then we 'went up' to Brussels.

I had 'inherited' a clapped-out car which had been mouldering in a garage. It was a Ford Taunus station wagon which had originally been white but was now no particular colour at all. The body was so rotten at the bottom that the exhaust fumes penetrated the interior. Summer and winter alike, the windows had to be left open, otherwise driver and passengers would have expired before they reached their destination.

I sometimes catered for 200 wedding guests and stuffed everything into the car. I had blue plates decorated with flowers, from a range which was being discontinued and which I had bought cheap. My mother had built up a stock of hundreds of Shell glasses. At the time, you received very nice glasses as a free gift every time you filled up your car with gas. And as there were several cars at home because we were a large family, the cupboards were stuffed full of these Shell glasses!

No one has hundreds of identical glasses. So we used Shell glasses at receptions in the homes of 'posh' people. I had bought a caterer's oven with foldaway handles, as on sedan chairs. So the oven, the gas cylinder, the plates, the Shell glasses and all the food were stuffed inside the car. The roof rack was also full. One day, when we arrived in Brussels, we realized that a crate of tomatoes and the crate of vegetables had fallen off somewhere along the highway! It was 9 pm. Looking out of the window, we saw that the neighbour had a vegetable garden. So we jumped over the wall and nicked some leeks from him. The funny thing is that like my father, I won a prize, for cooking.

I still had one last work placement to do and I chose Scheveneels, the best patisserie in Liège at the time. I spent three months there. I stayed in Liège to work at Café Robert, on Boulevard de la Sauvenière. Robert Lesenne was renowned. He prided himself on his contacts in the trade. He had promised to put in a good word for me with Roger Vergé, the famous chef at the Moulin de Mougins restaurant on the French riviera. A dream come true, or almost. The months went by and still no news from Mr Vergé. So I got out my smartest notepaper and wrote to all the great French chefs of the time, the Michelin three star chefs. With my résumé, I wrote a sort of covering letter, explaining why I wanted to work for them, which I photocopied 18 times. In the letter, I said that I was willing to work without pay for a year.

The extraordinary thing is that almost all of them replied, even if the answer was no. Just imagine what it's like for a young chef to open a letter embossed with the name of Paul Bocuse's restaurant.

To cut a long story short, I received three positive responses. First from Gérard Boyer in Rheims, then, at the same time, from Georges Blanc (La mère Blanc) in Vonnas and from Jo Rostand (La Bonne Auberge) in Antibes. In spring 1982, I found myself in Vonnas, in the Rhône-Alpes region of France. Georges Blanc paid guys like me €80 a month and paid for our accommodation at the young workers' hostel in Vonnas. He had been attracted by a line in my résumé which said that the Liège patisserie was "... one of the best in the kingdom of Belgium!", so I found myself employed as a pastry chef. At the end of the season, he suggested that I stay and offered to promote me and give me a pay rise. As I wanted to move on, he asked me which restaurant interested me. I said I would like to work with Michel Guérard; he picked up the telephone and got me a job there, in Eugénie-les-Bains. So at the end of the winter, in around February 1983, I found myself working at Michel Guérard's restaurant in the beautiful spa town of Eugénie-les-Bains in south west France. My first job there was pastries. In fact, chefs are definitely macho. Things are changing but most of the time they are not really bothered about desserts. In leading restaurants in the USA, for example, pastry chefs are often women.

I returned to New York at the end of the same year. In the meantime, I had been back to the USA twice, with my school. The geography teacher organized school trips for pupils. In 1978, we spent three months in the south, travelling through Florida, Louisiana, Mississippi and Tennessee. In 1979, we went to California, New Mexico, Nevada and Colorado.

I was fascinated by the United States. Come to think of it, I don't know whether 'fascination' is the right word. Like many things in life, everything happens by accident. My father had been persuaded to buy land in Florida, like lots of Belgians in the 1960s. The dollar had been very low at the time. He had really bought the land but there were some people who had been sold land which never existed.

My parents got a free trip to Florida and my father made Super 8 films. And it's true that when you see Miami like that for the first time, with canals, palm trees, huge houses, huge cars... And my father said that even the hotel's cleaner drove to work in a Cadillac! Even when you're only 4 or 5 years old, you're wide-eyed with wonder.

Working for Michel Guérard was what got me headed for America. The restaurant closed for 3 or 4 months every winter. People regularly called, looking for young private chefs to cook during the winter in the Caribbean or in the mountains, for example. A Belgian pal was ending his second season at Eugénie-les-Bains. The previous winter, he had worked in Switzerland for Princess Ira de Furstenberg. In late 1983, the same Ira de Furstenberg called this chef pal again and asked him to go to New York. Her partner's brother worked for an American bank in Switzerland. The president of the bank in New York had broken a leg when getting out of the bathtub and was wheelchair-bound. The Swiss staff wanted to send a private chef over as a gift for Thanksgiving. My pal had already found a job in California. He passed the phone to me and the first thing I was asked was: "How much do you want to earn?"

At the time, I was earning €350 a month for an 80-hour week. I asked for $2000 a month and started at $1500. Three weeks later, I found myself in a 800m2 apartment on Fifth Avenue in New York, with a guy who was boss of a bank with a staff of 17,000. He was single, having been divorced five times, loved Dewar's Scotch Whisky and ate only meat and potatoes.

I worked for him for a year and a half. I came back to Belgium every six months to renew my ...tourist visa. A year and a half later I went back to France, working for Alain Senderens in Paris for six or seven months. Then I did a two-week placement with Joël Robuchon, followed by a month in Milan with Gualtiero Marchesi, the first Michelin three star chef in Italian history.

Next I returned to the USA to work for the same banker. Three months later, I was 'poached' by a wealthy lady. Her father had started out as a messenger on Wall Street. Amongst other things, he had become the biggest stockholder in Columbia Pictures. At the time Forbes Magazine ranked them in sixth place amongst the wealthiest people in the USA.

My salary doubled. In 1985 and 1986, I earned $4000 a month, with board and lodging and even a car thrown in as part of the package. I had never really earned any money in my life. When you have always been virtually penniless, you react in one of two ways. Either you blow everything or you are reluctant to spend anything. My reaction was not to spend, I never even bought myself a $50 pair of shoes. It never even occurred to me to spend anything above that amount.

I worked mainly in New York. They had an apartment with 23 members of staff. A chauffeur, 3 butlers, 2 women who were responsible only for doing the laundry and ironing and a French dressmaker who only did alterations. Hubert de Givenchy came to the house for fitting sessions. On those days there was a small dinner. It involved a huge amount of work for me and no expense was spared: foie gras, truffles, caviar. There were monthly butcher's bills of $7000-8000.

I sometimes cooked joints of roast beef and 6-rib racks. The lady of the house only ate the slice in the middle, which had to be very rare but hot. When I had carved the joint, she drank the blood escaping from the cooked meat, in a glass. Her husband ate the two very well cooked outer slices. There was 5kg of meat left for the staff.

She sometimes asked for hamburgers and hot-dogs. At the age of 23 and having worked for Michel Guérard, one cannot help thinking "What a comedown..." But then you become a bit more relaxed. I remember that one day she wanted me to make an Indian dish for her, crab-filled pancakes. I analysed the recipe and managed to adapt it in a way that I found fun. It helped me to produce dishes which I would never even have considered if I had been left to my own devices.

In winter, we spent every weekend in the Bahamas. Sometimes we were there for two weeks. They had a gigantic house at Lyford Cay on the island of Nassau. I had five large local mamas to help me in the kitchen and go to the local market. They taught me how to add exactly the right amount of extremely hot chillies!

The maître d' was English. He was the Spencer family's former butler and claimed to have been involved in the upbringing of the future Princess Diana. My employer had hired him to recount anecdotes about Diana, the royal family and English high society. He was really talented in an over-the-top sort of way. He was the star of the society evenings. The guests came to enjoy my cooking but were much more interested in the show put on by this maître d' who had missed his calling as an actor. I remember a dinner given for Michael Caine's birthday, at which Sean Connery, Laura Ashley and Mr and Mrs Cadbury were guests. The cake was a duo of white and dark chocolate, dusted with bitter cocoa. When Michael Caine blew out his 50 candles, our super butler and his white dinner jacket were covered in cocoa!

In early 1987, I spent $2000 on a round-the-world ticket in the Bahamas, with New York as the first stop. I took all my cases and left them in Belgium. Then I set out for Amsterdam, Bangkok and Sydney... on my own, with just a backpack.

Bombe au chocolat (chocolat mousse cake)

SERVES 6-8:

400G PLAIN DARK CHOCOLATE, 60CL FRESH WHIPPING CREAM (35% FAT),
50G GROUNDNUT OR SUNFLOWER OIL.

FOR THE ALMOND BISCUIT (COOKIE) DISC (TO BE PREPARED THE DAY BEFORE):
100G EGG WHITES (2-3 EGGS ACCORDING TO SIZE), 50G CASTER (SUPERFINE) SUGAR,
50G ICING (CONFECTIONERS') SUGAR, 100G GROUND ALMONDS, 1 TBSP FLOUR.

FOR THE MOULD: BUTTER, FLOUR.

FOR THE FINISH: BITTER COCOA.

ON THE FIRST DAY:
- Preheat the oven to 160°C.
- Thoroughly mix the caster sugar and the icing sugar to ensure that the latter does not form lumps. Leave to rest.
- Mix the ground almonds with half the sugar and the tablespoon of flour.
- Whisk the egg whites until they are not too stiff, adding half the sugar towards the end. Blend the almond mixture into the egg whites without stirring too much.
- Grease and flour a 20cm non-stick mould. Turn it over to remove the excess flour.
- Pour in the almond biscuit mixture. Bake at 160°C for 20 minutes.
- Leave to cool on a wire rack.

ON THE SECOND DAY:
Continue preparation of the Bombe au chocolat.
- Line a hemispherical stainless steel or earthenware bowl with food film. In this bowl, the top of the chocolate mixture has to fit the diameter of the almond biscuit disc, i.e. 20cm.
- Melt the chocolate and the oil in a bain-marie. Heat to 50°C.
- Take the cream out of the refrigerator (it needs to be well chilled).
- Half whip it, until it barely holds in the whisk, like for Irish coffee.
- Add a third of the cream to the melted chocolate and mix with a flexible rubber spatula for 20 seconds. Add the rest of the cream and blend it in with the spatula, lifting the preparation.
  This operation should take only 10 seconds. Pour this mixture into the bowl and place the génoise biscuit disc on top. Refrigerate overnight.
- Remove from the mould and take off the film. Dust with bitter cocoa.
- To slice, dip a sharp knife in hot water and do so again after cutting each slice.

Lemon tart

Sablé pastry dough needs to be well chilled to make it easier to roll out. As it is comparatively fragile, the advice that the lump of dough be placed between two plastic sheets is sometimes given.

The purpose of lining with melted white chocolate a prebaked pastry base, later to be filled, is simply to create a thin waterproof film, preventing the baked pastry from becoming moist and consequently crumbly.

Any pastry left over can be stored, if carefully wrapped, for one or two weeks in the refrigerator or for a few months in the freezer. If the pastry has been frozen, bring it back to room temperature by leaving it in the refrigerator overnight.

If you prefer a less 'lemony' flavour, substitute orange juice for a quarter or a half of the lemon juice. There are other variants, such as substituting lime for lemon. In a Caribbean version, replace the lemon juice with fresh pineapple juice, plus a handful of grated coconut and two tablespoons of "Rhum Vieux" (aged rum).

SERVES 6-8:

FOR THE CREAM: 190G LIQUID FRESH CREAM, 150G SUGAR, 15CL FRESHLY SQUEEZED LEMON JUICE, 90G FULL-FAT FROMAGE BLANC, PEEL OF 1/2 LEMON, 2 WHOLE EGGS, 3 EGG YOLKS.

FOR THE SABLÉ PASTRY : 200G BUTTER, 150G ICING (CONFECTIONERS') SUGAR, 1 EGG WHITE, PEEL OF 1 LEMON, 60G FLAKED ALMONDS, 1 PINCH SALT, 300G FLOUR.

FOR THE FINISH: 30G WHITE CHOCOLATE.

- Preheat the oven to 160°C.
- Put all the pastry ingredients, except the egg, into the food processor with the paddle attachment. Blend for 1 minute to produce a sablé pastry mixture. Add the egg and mix for a further 20 seconds.
- Form a ball with the dough and wrap in food film. Refrigerate for at least 2 hours.
- For one tart, allow 250-300g of well chilled pastry. Flour the working surface. Use a rolling pin to flatten the pastry until it is 4-5mm thick. Line a 22-24cm in diameter pie dish (tart pan) with a removable base with the pastry. Cover the pastry with baking paper, fill with dried beans and bake blind at 160°C for 25 minutes. Take out of the oven, remove the beans and the paper and bake for a further 5 minutes to dry the pastry.
- Leave to cool and brush the inside of the pastry base with a thin layer of white chocolate melted in a bain-marie beforehand.
- Put all the ingredients of the lemon cream in a food processor bowl and blend. Whiz for 20 seconds. Strain through a conical strainer to remove any lumps.
- Pour into a small thick-bottomed pan and heat up over a medium heat, stirring continuously with a wooden spoon until the mixture reaches 92-93°C. When the mixture starts to thicken, remove the pan from the heat while continuing to stir. Pour into the pastry base, still in its mould.
- Leave to rest on the table for 5 minutes, without moving or disturbing the tart. Carefully transfer it to the refrigerator for at least an hour.
- Ideally, the lemon tart should be eaten the same day.

Pecan tart

Low-fat fromage frais can be used but full-fat cheese obviously produces a creamier result.
The mixture and the pecan nuts can be baked on their own, without a pastry base, in individual portions, in a ramekin dish, a Catalan cream custard mould or, even better, a lightly greased non-stick mould. When baked, turn out of the moulds.

Muscovado sugar is produced from whole, concentrated sugar cane syrup, which is then dried and not centrifuged. The word muscovado comes from the Spanish word "mascabado", meaning 'unrefined'. This type of sugar is therefore rich in a variety of minerals.

SERVES 6-8:

125-150G NET PECAN NUTS (SHELLED), 1 SABLÉ PASTRY BASE (SEE RECIPE PREVIOUS PAGE).

FOR THE FILLING: 200G LIQUID FRESH CREAM, 100G SMOOTH FROMAGE BLANC, 2 EGGS, 2 EGG YOLKS, 100G MUSCOVADO SUGAR, 1 TSP NATURAL VANILLA EXTRACT.

- Preheat the oven to 200°C.
- Break the meat of the nuts into 4 lobes and arrange them in a single layer on the tart base.
- Put all the ingredients in the filling into a large bowl. Whip for 30 seconds, without causing the mixture to froth. Pour it onto the nuts.
- Bake first for 10 minutes at 200°C, then for a further 10 minutes at 140°C.

Apple tartlets

Fructose can be substituted for sugar. As fructose is a more powerful sweetener than conventional sugar, it produces the same sweet taste but with fewer calories.

Virgin vegetable oil can also be substituted for butter, reducing the saturated fats content. If vegetable oil is used, the amount of flour in the almond cream preparation needs to be increased slightly (count 20g).

If you wish to prepare this recipe in advance, you can freeze the little tarts raw and bake them as and when required. They will of course take longer to bake.

Apples can be replaced with seasonal fruits, such as peaches or plums, halved and skin side facing down. Sprinkle with icing sugar so that the tartlets will be nicely coloured.

MAKES 6:

3-4 GRANNY SMITH OR GOLDEN DELICIOUS APPLES, 30G ICING (CONFECTIONERS') SUGAR.

FOR THE ALMOND CREAM: 125G GROUND ALMONDS, 125G SUGAR OR FRUCTOSE, 125G CHILLED BUTTER, CUBED, PINCH OF SALT, 1 TSP NATURAL VANILLA EXTRACT, 50G FLOUR, 2 LARGE EGGS, PEEL OF 1/4 LEMON, JUICE OF 1/2 LEMON.

- Put the almonds, the sugar, the butter, the salt, the flour, the vanilla extract and the lemon peel in the food processor bowl. Blend for 1 minute, using the paddle attachment, until the mixture is of the consistency of fine sand.
- Add the eggs and the lemon juice. Blend for a further 20 seconds.
- Set aside this almond cream – the future filling – in a bowl.
- Refrigerate for at least 30 minutes. This almond cream will keep for several days in the refrigerator.
- Preheat the oven to 175°C.

- Wash and wipe the apples. Cut into 8 quarters without peeling. Remove the pips (seeds) and their membranes.
- Place baking paper cups on a muffin tray. Fill them two-thirds full with almond cream. On the surface of the cream, place a few apple quarters. Dust with icing sugar and bake at 175°C for 20-25 minutes
- Serve at room temperature or slightly warm.

Apricot tartlets

MAKES 6:

ALMOND CREAM (SEE RECIPE PREVIOUS PAGE), 12 APRICOTS,
30G ICING (CONFECTIONERS') SUGAR.

- Preheat the oven to 175°C.
- Place baking paper cups on a muffin tray. Fill them two-thirds full with almond cream.
- On the surface of the cream, place 4 good quality canned apricot halves or fresh apricot halves, ripe but firm. Dust with icing sugar and bake at 175°C for 20-25 minutes. You can also bake a large family-sized tart. If so, bake for 30 minutes, taking care to lower the heat if the surface is colouring too quickly.
- For more pronounced colouring, put the tartlets under the grill for 1-2 minutes after baking.

In season, add a few fresh lavender flowers to the almond cream, allowing one flower for 6 people.

NY cheese cake

SERVES 12:

FOR THE CREAM: 4 EGGS, 2 EGG YOLKS, 600G CREAM CHEESE
(PHILADELPHIA, KIRI OR SAINT MORET, FOR EXAMPLE), 250G SUGAR OR FRUCTOSE,
50G PASTRY FLOUR, 1 TSP NATURAL VANILLA EXTRACT, PINCH OF SALT.
FOR THE BISCUIT BASE: 12 PETIT BEURRE BISCUITS, CRUSHED, 50G MELTED BUTTER.

To remove from the mould, slide the wet tip (plunged into hot water) of the blade of a knife around the vertical sides of the mould. Turn out carefully and place on a large dish. Decorate with strawberries or raspberries and serve with a red berry coulis or a slightly runny jam or jelly.

- Preheat the oven to 200°C. Mix together the sugar, the pinch of salt and the flour. Sieve and put into the food processor with the beater. Blend with the cheese, whisking for 1 minute. Add the whole eggs, the egg yolks and the vanilla. Blend quickly to obtain a smooth and homogenous cream.
- To assemble: Take a high-sided round mould, grease lightly and place a disc of baking paper, cut to fit the size of the mould exactly, inside.
- Using a spatula, mix the crushed "Petit Beurre" biscuit crumbs with the tepid melted butter.
- Pour into the mould and press down firmly so that the base is uniformly covered. Pour the cheese cream into the mould and bake at a temperature of 200°C for 10 minutes. Lower the oven temperature to 140°C and bake for a further 35 minutes.
- Leave to cool for 30 minutes, then refrigerate for 12 hours, still in the mould.

Carré du mendiant (Dried fruit and nut squares)

SERVES 8:

200G EGG WHITES (6-7 EGGS), 120G CASTER (SUPERFINE) SUGAR, 120G ICING (CONFECTIONERS') SUGAR, 200G GROUND ALMONDS, 25G PASTRY FLOUR (3 TBSP), PINCH OF SALT, 65G WHOLE ALMONDS, WITH THE SKIN, 65G WHOLE HAZELNUTS, WITH THE SKIN, 65G WALNUTS, 80G BLACK RAISINS, 25G PISTACHIOS OR PINE NUTS.

Slicing this frozen cake means that the squares are geometrically shaped, while the texture is soft and chewy. Once cut, store the squares in an airtight tin at room temperature.

The almond mixture can be flavoured with orange and lemon peel.

As a variant, this cake can be made with walnuts and coffee. To do so, add two tablespoons of very finely ground coffee to the mixture before baking.

For a 'healthy' variant, substitute fructose for regular sugar and you have a pastry which contains no cholesterol or glucose but is rich in dried fruit and nut oils.

- Preheat the oven to 190°C.
- Carefully mix together the caster sugar and the icing sugar.
- Thoroughly mix the ground almonds with half of the two sugars mixture, the flour and the pinch of salt.
- Whisk the egg whites until they are not too stiff, which should take 30 seconds. Then blend in the remainder of the sugars mixture.
- When the egg whites are ready, add the ground almonds-based mixture, blending quickly. The mixture should not be too smooth and homogeneous.
- Mixed together all the dried fruits and nuts and place them in a square baking tin (pan), covered with baking paper. The baking tin must be large enough to allow the dried fruits and nuts to form a regular, densely packed layer, so that the almond mixture will not drip through onto the bottom. If necessary, fill in any gaps with extra dried fruits and nuts.
- Carefully pour the almond mixture over the dried fruits and nuts, ensuring that they do not move. Smooth the mixture delicately using a spatula and bake at 190°C for 35-40 minutes.
- After taking out of the oven, leave to cool at room temperature for 20 minutes and freeze in the baking tin for 12 hours.
- Turn out of the mould and cut into neat squares, using a sharp knife.

Red berry crumble

SERVES 6:

400-500G MIXED RED BERRIES: BLACKCURRANTS, RED CURRANTS, RASPBERRIES, BLUEBERRIES, BLACKBERRIES, ETC.

FOR THE CRUMBLE: 24 PETIT BEURRE BISCUITS, 100G FRUCTOSE, 1/2 TSP POWDERED CINNAMON, 40G BUTTER.

Crumble can easily be made outside the red berries season. To do so, freeze them in appropriate portions when they are at their peak in terms of ripeness and taste. Specialist food retailers also stock excellent frozen mixtures of red berries.

- Preheat the oven to 225°C.
- Roughly crush 12 "Petit Beurre" biscuits with a fork, then divide them out, in 6 small individual gratin dishes or 6 ramekin dishes. Place the mixed red berries on this first layer of biscuits.
- In a bowl, roughly crush the remaining 12 "Petit Beurre" biscuits with a fork. Mix them with the fructose, the cinnamon and the melted butter.
- Divide the mixture out in the dishes, above the fruit.
- Bake at 225°C for 15 minutes.

Crème brûlée and caramel tart

SERVES 6-8:

FOR THE CREAM: 50CL FRESH CREAM, 4 EGG YOLKS, 1/2 VANILLA POD, 1 WHOLE EGG, 60G SUGAR.

FOR THE SOFT CARAMEL: 75G SUGAR, 75G FRESH CREAM, 80G WHITE CHOCOLATE, 1 SABLÉ PASTRY BASE (SEE RECIPE, PAGE 44)

- Preheat the oven to 110°C.
- Split the vanilla pod lengthwise. Scrape out the seeds with a small paring knife. Put in a small pan with the fresh cream and bring to the boil. Remove the vanilla pod.
- Break the whole egg into a large bowl, add the yolks and sugar and mix with a wooden spoon. Pour in the boiling cream in two stages. To avoid 'cooking' the eggs, first raise the temperature with a quarter of the cream. Mix with the spoon and add the rest.
- Strain through a conical strainer and pour onto the pastry base.
- Bake at 110°C for 15-20 minutes.
- Leave to rest at room temperature for 20 minutes, then refrigerate. Melt the 80g white chocolate in a bain-marie.
- Put the sugar in a frying pan or pan, turn up the heat so that the dry heat caramelizes it, turning it light brown in colour. Lower the temperature by adding the fresh cream. When the mixture has cooled down and is tepid, add the white chocolate and whisk to produce a smooth and homogeneous caramel.
- Pour onto the well chilled tart to form a 3mm coating. Smooth and level out with a flat metal spatula.

Lemon spéculoos

MAKES **60:**

210G CHILLED BUTTER, 300G PASTRY FLOUR, 210G DEMERARA SUGAR,
1 TSP POWDERED CINNAMON, PEEL OF 1 LEMON, PINCH SALT, 1 EGG, JUICE OF 1/4 LEMON,
150G FLAKED ALMONDS.

To keep these biscuits (cookies) fresh, they can be deep-frozen in a tightly sealed freezer bag and taken out of the freezer as required. Deep-freezing means that when removed from the freezer they are just as delicious as when freshly baked.

The pastry balls can also be deep-frozen and the spéculoos can be sliced and baked as required. This 'home' bake-off method results in incomparably fresh products.

- The day before, put the butter, cut into cubes, the flour, the demerara sugar, the cinnamon, the lemon peel and the salt into the food processor bowl. Using the paddle attachment, mix for approximately 30 seconds to produce a sablé (rich short crust/sugar crust) pastry mixture.
- Add the egg and the lemon juice and blend for 10 seconds. Transfer to a large mixing bowl and add the flaked almonds, mixing gently with a spatula to minimize breakage of the almonds. Place two sheets of alumin(i)um foil, 20-25cm long, on the worktop (counter). Place half of the pastry in the middle of each. Roll up the foil to form two regular sausage-shaped parcels. Refrigerate for at least 12 hours.
- The following day, preheat the oven to a temperature of 140°-150°C.
- Unwrap the pastry parcels and cut them into regular thin slices, 3-4mm thick. Place them on a baking tray covered with baking paper. Bake for approximately 12-15 minutes.
- Leave to cool for 10 minutes, then immediately transfer the spéculoos to an airtight tin (Tupperware, for example) to ensure that they stay dry and crispy.

Pistachio, olive oil and lemon peel biscotti

Biscotti – like the British English word 'biscuit', derived from old French, itself derived from Latin – literally means 'baked twice', which makes sense in this particular recipe.

Like glucose, fructose is present in fruit and honey. Chemically, they are both exactly the same. But the structure of their atoms is different. Fructose is metabolized by our bodies more slowly than other sugars.
It is the sweetest of all the common sugars. In cold drinks – only – just half the amount is required to obtain the same sweetness as with 'normal' sugar, meaning that the calorie intake is lower. However, this remarkable sweetening power returns to normal in hot drinks. Opt for fruit fructose, as there is also fructose synthesized from glucose.

The use of virgin oil is designed to make these biscuits/cookies light and easily digestible.

MAKES 30:

6CL EXTRA VIRGIN OLIVE OIL, 350G FLOUR, 150G FRUCTOSE, 2 WHOLE EGGS, 2G SALT, 5G BICARBONATE OF SODA, 180G GREEN PISTACHIOS, UNSALTED AND UNROASTED, PEEL OF ONE LEMON, PEEL OF ONE ORANGE, 3 TBSP LEMON JUICE, 1 TBSP NATURAL VANILLA EXTRACT.

FOR THE FINISH: FRUCTOSE.

- Preheat the oven to 150°C.
- Put all the ingredients, apart from the pistachios, in the food processor bowl. Whiz with the paddle attachment for 30 seconds. Transfer the dough to a large mixing bowl and add the pistachios.
- Knead the dough to blend in the pistachios. Form two 20cm-long sausage shapes and roll them in the fructose, so that they are covered by a crystal crust.
- Place them on a baking tray covered with baking paper. Flatten them slightly and bake for 35 minutes.
- Remove from the oven and leave to cool for 10 minutes. Cut the sausage shapes into oblique slices 15mm thick and return to the oven for 8-10 minutes to ensure that the biscotti dry out.

Ginger snaps

MAKES **80:**

250G CHILLED BUTTER, 875G PASTRY FLOUR, 900G MUSCOVADO SUGAR, 4G POWDERED
GINGER, 2G POWDERED CLOVES, 2G POWDERED CARDAMON, 2G POWDERED CINNAMON,
2G SALT, 20G BICARBONATE OF SODA, 5 WHOLE EGGS, 3 TBSP WHITE WINE VINEGAR.

FOR THE FINISH: COARSE GRANULATED SUGAR

The powdered ginger can be replaced by 20g of fresh ginger, cut into minute cubes.

If you want your biscuits (cookies) to be paler in colour, you can mix the types of sugar, using half muscovado and half caster (superfine) sugar.

- Preheat the oven to 150°C.
- Put all the ingredients except the eggs and the vinegar into the food processor bowl and whiz for 30 seconds. Add the eggs and vinegar and whiz for a further 15 seconds.
- Remove the dough and put it into a mixing bowl. Mix with a spatula until it becomes smooth and homogenized. As the dough is rather sticky, form small regular balls using a small ice cream scoop, dipping it in hot water between each ball.
- Next put the balls into a large bowl filled with granulated sugar. Rolls the balls round so that they are well coated with the sugar.
- Put them on a baking tray, covered with baking paper, spacing them 6cm.apart.
- Flatten them slightly (up to 1.5cm in height), pressing on them with moistened finger tips, then bake them at 150°C for 12 minutes. The ginger snaps should still be slightly soft when removed from the oven.
- When they have cooled down, store them in an airtight tin.

Brownies

These brownies can be decorated with two or three walnut halves placed on the dough before baking.

A brownie can be reheated in a microwave oven for 5 seconds before serving. For a slightly more sophisticated and richer dessert, serve with a scoop of traditionally made vanilla ice cream or Chantilly cream.

Brownies keep for two months in the freezer in a hermetically sealed freezer bag.

MAKES ENOUGH FOR **10-15** PEOPLE:

250G PLAIN DARK CHOCOLATE, 250G BUTTER, 250G WHOLE EGGS (4-5 ACCORDING TO SIZE), 250G CASTER (SUPERFINE), 25G PASTRY FLOUR (3 TBSP).

- Preheat the oven to 140°C.
- Roughly chop the chocolate into pieces Transfer to a medium-sized pan with the butter. Heat in a bain-marie, in simmering water, until the two ingredients have melted. Mix well. Transfer to a large bowl.
- Using a spatula, add the sieved flour and the sugar, mixed together beforehand. Add the whole eggs and mix. Leave to rest for 30 minutes.
- Place in small individual moulds covered with a paper cup, either the ready-made commercially available variety or home-made from baking paper. Bake at 140°C for 25 minutes (60-70g) brownies or for 35 minutes (90-120g brownies). As the butter and chocolate content of these brownies is very high, they keep perfectly for a week if stored in a metal tin at room temperature.

Liège waffles with pearl sugar

SERVES 12:

FOR THE SOURDOUGH: (TO PREPARE 12 HOURS IN ADVANCE) 150G FLOUR, 10CL WATER, 10G BAKER'S YEAST.

FOR THE PASTRY/BATTER: 350G FLOUR, 250G BUTTER, 50G CASTER (SUPERFINE) SUGAR, 250G EGGS (4-5 ACCORDING TO SIZE), 2 DL MILK, 5G SALT, 1 TSP NATURAL VANILLA EXTRACT, 10G BAKER'S YEAST, 250G PEARL SUGAR.

- For the sourdough: mix together all the ingredients to produce a supple and homogenous dough. Put in a bowl, covered with plastic film, and leave to rest at room temperature, i.e. at least 20°C, for a minimum of 12 hours.

- For the pastry/batter: put the flour, butter, eggs, vanilla and sourdough into the beater bowl. Knead with the dough hook at low speed. Add the yeast, mixed in the tepid milk. Blend for 1 minute, then add the salt and the caster sugar. Knead at high speed until the pastry/batter becomes detached from the bowl, which should take 5-7 minutes.

- Add the pearl sugar. Mix quickly, for 30 seconds, leave the pastry/batter to rest for 20 minutes, then cut into 120g lumps. Put them on a lightly greased sheet and cover with a damp cloth. Leave the lumps of dough to rise at room temperature (at least 20°C) for 20-30 minutes.

- Meanwhile, preheat the clean waffle-maker and cook the waffles until they are nicely coloured, which should take 2-3 minutes. Grease the waffle-maker's surface with a neutral oil before making each waffle. Leave to cool on a wire rack.

Pain d'épices (Gingerbread)

SERVES 12:

500G RYE FLOUR, 500G HONEY, 35CL WATER, 1 HEAPED TSP BICARBONATE OF SODA,
1 TSP GROUND ANISEED, 1 TSP GROUND CINNAMON, 1/2 TSP CRUSHED CLOVE, BUTTER.

The mix of spices in this traditional recipe varies. However, powdered ginger is invariably used – and sometimes nutmeg.

- Preheat the oven to 180°C.
- Put the water into a pan and bring to the boil. Remove from the heat and dissolve the honey in the water.
- Pour this hot mixture onto the flour and the spices. Mix immediately until a smooth paste forms.
- Grease a 1kg loaf tin (pan) and pour the mixture into it.
- Bake at 160-180°C for approximately 1 hour.

Manhattan choc chip cookies

MAKES 8:

185G CHILLED BUTTER, 125G CASTER (SUPERFINE) SUGAR, 125G LIGHT-COLOURED
SOFT BROWN SUGAR, 270G PASTRY FLOUR, 3G SALT (1/2 TSP), 3G BICARBONATE OF
SODA (1/2 TSP), 1 WHOLE EGG, 1 EGG YOLK, 1/2 TSP NATURAL VANILLA EXTRACT,
250G PLAIN DARK CHOCOLATE CHIPS.

- Preheat the oven to 150°C.
- Put the caster sugar, the soft brown sugar, the flour, the salt and
  the bicarbonate of soda in a food processor bowl with the paddle
  attachment. Blend for 1 minute to produce a mixture of the consistency of fine sand. Add the eggs and the vanilla extract. Blend
  for 20 seconds.
- When the mixture is smooth and homogenous, add the chocolate chips. To bake, weigh out 110-120g balls of dough. Place on
  trays covered with greaseproof paper or special baking paper. Flatten each piece of dough with (moistened) fingertips to produce
  roughly regular circles approximately 18cm in diameter. Bake at
  150°C for 20 minutes.
- If you are unable to find chocolate chips or drops, roughly chop
  with a knife a bar of plain dark chocolate.

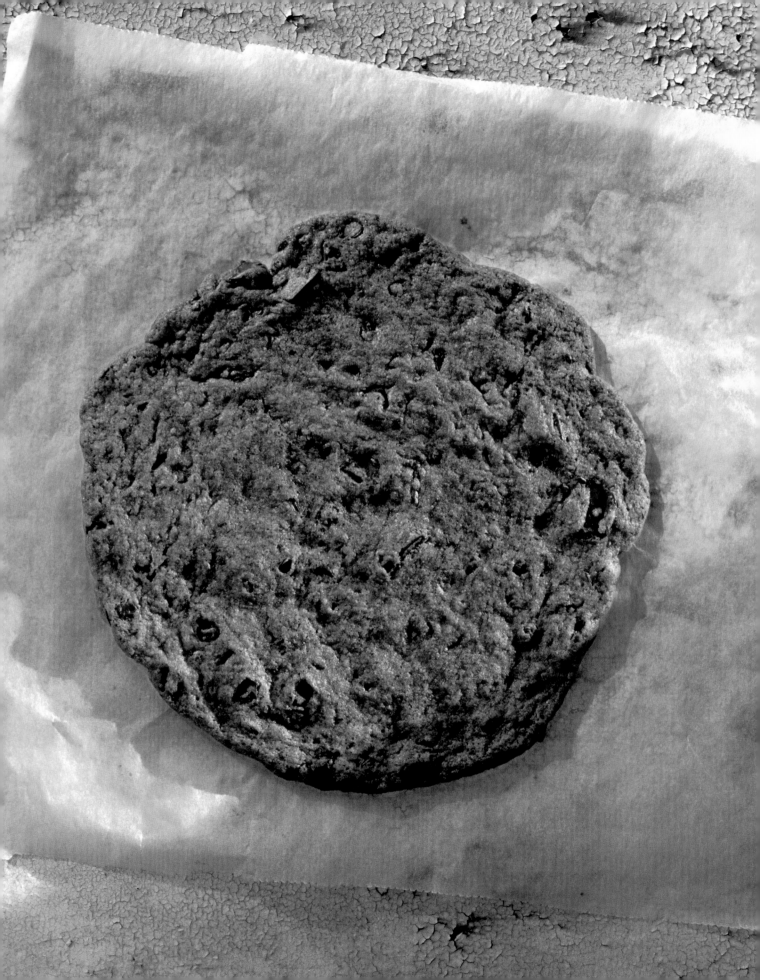

The first bread

I didn't start making bread to fulfil some long-cherished dream. It all came about by chance, as opportunities happened to arise, and, most importantly, at a given moment, because I got into a line of business which I find very satisfying.

The name Le Pain Quotidien came from something my father said during an ordinary conversation. At one point he exclaimed: "Moi ce n'est pas mon pain quotidien ! " (literally "It's not my daily bread!" but meaning that it's not one of your usual habits). I remembered the expression and a few weeks later gave this name with its biblical overtones to a business I was setting up.

Let's go back to the beginning of the story. I was the chef of Le Café du Dôme and as such ordered bread. Initially, I obtained my supplies from two leading bakeries in Brussels, although I was not really bowled over by the type of bread which they could offer me.

On the other hand, I distinctly remembered Poilâne bread, which was served at L'Archestrate, Alain Senderens's restaurant. The freshly baked round loaf went with the cheese course. The leftovers, the bread from the day before, were for the staff's meals. I had really got to like the taste of this bread and would have given a lot to find it again.

Poilâne bread was distributed in Belgium but sporadically, in a few upmarket delis. So I needed to find an independent and speedy source to obtain daily supplies. A new Belgian courier service company – called Paris Bruxelles Express – could do the job. Apparently they were always laden on the outward trip to Paris but came back to Brussels carrying relatively little.

I met Lionel Poilâne at his shop on rue du Cherche-Midi in Paris. He was immediately very nice, open and positive about my request. We worked out a precise scenario. The van would collect the warm bread at 5 pm every afternoon. There would be one invoice a month. He gave me a copy of his book as I left. Everything was simple.

In appearance only, as we had not thought things through sufficiently, in the sense that we had reckoned without all the red tape. In the late 1980s, Europe's borders were not yet open. Every time the courier service crossed the border, the driver would have had to complete customs papers and pay €40 in charges, which was more than the price of the 6 or 8 loaves carried.

It was at that time that I bought two dilapidated properties. I was not especially keen to become a property owner, but it was too good an opportunity to miss.

Once again, chance came into play, one day in January 1990 when I decided to fit my car with snow tyres. I found a garage not very far from the restaurant, on the other side of the North Station. It was supposedly a development area. In the 1960s, there had been a large-scale project to build a World Trade Center with 'skyscrapers' ten or so storeys high. The whole district had been demolished but there had been only vague attempts at regeneration. The Manhattan of Brussels was more like a derelict construction site. Apart from two or three towers and the President WTC Hotel – a somewhat incongruous long bar shape – nothing else had been built.

It would take the garage mechanic half an hour to change the tyres. I killed time by going to the nearest café, at the corner of a street, on place Gaucheret, and ordering a coffee. It was a winter day, the light was magnificent. I really had the impression that I was back in Manhattan. The waste land, the run-down houses and the towers, defiant in their solitude, in my eyes that was New York, the Bronx, the ghetto, all at once.

There was a 'For Sale' sign on the bay windows of the café. I immediately dialled the number given. The asking price was €125,000 for the two properties, with shop space at ground level and 12 apartments. As I was a tenant, the only thing I was interested in was converting the top floor into a penthouse, with a 100m2 hanging garden, with the added advantage of being down town, right in the centre of the city, and a stone's throw from my restaurant. That's when things took off. The realtor told me straightaway that he could help me to finance the operation. He put me in touch with a small discount bank. Almost no cash had to be paid up front!

In addition, the government of the city of Brussels was granting renovation subsidies which, given that the district was in a sorry state of repair, could be as much as 60% of the building work budget.

Everything was too perfect. I would be able to rent out the refurbished apartments. The operation promised to be financially profitable, very profitable in fact.

But what to do with the shop space at ground level in a down-at-heel district? The idea of a bakery appeared to me as the Virgin Mary did to Bernadette in Lourdes. I set up Le Pain Quotidien as what is known in Europe as a limited liability company (a sort of joint-stock company) with two stockholders: my father's second wife and a textile merchant for whom I occasionally provided catering services.

Each of us paid up €12,500. The company's capital – €37,500 – was to be used to renovate the commercial part, i.e. the bake house as such in the basement and a bakery with a few tables to serve snacks at ground floor level. A bank had agreed to a leasing arrangement so that I could buy the oven and the kneading machine, two essential items of equipment.

Then, in the middle of the demolition work, everything collapsed – literally! The architect had planned to make an opening, to create a single space in the future bakery. The party wall between the two buildings gave way, bringing down with it the five floors of the storeys and the roof. My two houses literally imploded. All that was left was the outer carcase of the building.

Almost the entire capital of Le Pain Quotidien company had been swallowed up in the place. We were left penniless. And the leased equipment had been ordered and was due to arrive two months later.

All I found to house it was the back of a garage near the national livestock market in Anderlecht, another district of Brussels. It belonged to Lebanese second-hand car dealers. Given the urgency, it was a real godsend, especially as I could use a fuel oil tank. So the oven and the kneading machine were installed. We started out with nothing. The water supply came from a single hosepipe. I used a compressor to disinfect the former spare parts shelves, which were now to be used for bread. I bought a paint spray and painted everything – walls and ceilings – white. To get started, I still needed a table and the famous wicker bread baskets, lined with linen, in which to leave the sourdough bread to rise, something I had seen in Lionel Poilâne's book.

I could therefore make bread for Le Café du Dôme. But baking 6-8 loaves a day with such large facilities seemed like a tiny order. I couldn't afford to take it on. So I rented the store at 16 rue Antoine Dansaert, right next to a fairly upmarket jazzy bar called L'Archiduc, paying a monthly rent of €650 and investing €15,000 in refurbishment. The district, opposite the Brussels Stock Exchange was promising. Several young fashion designers and a few interior decorators had recently moved in. If I were looking for trendy customers, it was definitely the place to be. But I was penniless!

Financial sleight of hand was the only solution. The store had been financed with the balance of the mortgage on the place Gaucheret properties, in fact the sums which had not yet been paid up. I sent to the bank the invoices of the plumber, the electrician, the painter Norberte, etc., who were working on the rue Antoine Dansaert property. No one ever realized that the paperwork on the two business ventures had been mixed up and I repaid the mortgage regularly and promptly.

When my line of credit at the bank was exhausted, the trades people agreed to continue working and to await the opening to be paid. For two months, perhaps three, they came by every evening and I paid them back at a rate of €25 or €30, from the day's takings.

Naturally, the bakery had had to be fitted out with furniture. Near the flea market, there was a large store, a sort of warehouse specializing in pine furniture. That was where I found the first large table, measuring 3.82 metres by 1.12 metres. The common table, one of the characteristic features of Le Pain Quotidien experience, had come into being. Fifteen years later, it still has pride of place in the rue Dansaert store. Folding chairs, of the type used on open air terraces, which had been recovered from a brewery's stocks, were placed round the table.

I bought an old counter and an old-fashioned bread rack. The chrome shelves in the window came from an Arab bakery near Sainte-Marie church in Brussels. The round loaves were sliced on a butcher's block, bought from a representative who had succeeded in persuading me that this sort of utensil was essential. The loaves were weighed on my grandfather's old Berkel weighing scales – which, incidentally, are still being used in the same store!

Broadly speaking, everything which was instrumental in subsequently forming the image and the signature of Le Pain Quotidien was already present in this first store. The large jam/jelly cabinet had been constructed from pallet wood. The glass partitions had been removed from the doors. This was not because we were seeking to be original but quite simply for the sake of commercial efficiency, to grab more easily what constituted our embryonic grocery business. We sold the jams/jellies which were served at breakfast, traditionally made upmarket products. At the time, back in 1990, wild strawberry jam/jelly cost €6.50 a jar. The regular strawberry variety was €4. Apricot was the cheapest, at just over €2 a jar. And a 2kg loaf cost €4.90.

At the outset, the only types of bread sold were a wheat loaf and a 1.2kg walnut loaf, made with 1kg of the same dough and 200g of walnuts. And there was also a rye loaf. They were distinguished by what is called the 'baker's signature', the 'slashes' made on the surface of the dough just before it goes into the oven.

Croissants and rolls were not served. The only three cakes which could be bought to take out or could be eaten on the spot were made at Le Café du Dôme, where I still had the status of consultant. They were the à la carte desserts served in the restaurant: Bombe au chocolat, Lemon Tart and Pecan Tart, a recipe that I had brought back from the USA.

We didn't even have a refrigerated counter. Only tarts freshly made that day were displayed. As the Bombe au chocolat was too fragile, a plaster cast model, dusted with cocoa, was on display instead of the real thing. A young student who had just started work in the store managed to sell the plaster cast cake...

My experience with the book "Minceur exquise", which had been published in the UK and the USA in the meantime, made me realize the importance of the media. So I asked Brigitte Forissier, Robert Laffont's press attaché for Belgium, whether she would get the troops out again for the inauguration of my rue Dansaert venture. On Thursday October 26 1990, the day of the opening, I ate 26 breakfasts, 26 coffees, 26 bread and jam. Between 7 am and 11 am, 26 journalists had breakfast in succession!

At the time I had no delivery vehicle. I delivered the bread in my own car, a green BMW convertible. The loaves arrived at the store in flour bags, which was my way of recycling the latter. The following Saturday, I arrived at the store with the morning's second delivery. It was full of people. So I helped the team out in dealing with this sudden rush. Sandwiches had to be prepared, coffees served, etc. What a hubbub – amplified by our second-hand slicer which was missing three blades. It made such a noise that we had nicknamed it 'the grandmother'.

I had forgotten my car, which was parked in the street where it should not have been. Logically enough, it had been taken away by a tow truck. An hour later – it was already 9.30 am – I wanted to go and get my car back from the city's central police station, called L'Amigo, located behind city hall nearby.

No need to describe the atmosphere, with the waiting room, the desk officer on duty reading his newspaper, Le Soir, the newspaper par excellence of the French-speaking citizens of Brussels. Then I spotted the front page headline: "Give us our daily bread!" I could hardly believe my eyes.

Le Soir was talking about me, about Le Pain Quotidien! I ran to rue Dansaert, I dropped everything, the formalities and my convertible. At that moment, 25 people were standing in line outside the store. They were all there to buy the Daily Bread. By 10 am we had run out of bread. We suggested that customers come back in the afternoon. At 5 pm, we were there with 48 freshly baked, still warm wheat loaves. Many of the customers who had been disappointed in the morning came back to rue Dansaert in the afternoon, as we had suggested. And the second batch of loaves sold in 20 minutes.

Since then, we have always been rushed off our feet, '7 days a week, 365 days a year' …

Fromage blanc, radish and spring onion (scallion) tartine

FOR 4 PORTIONS:

4 LARGE SLICES OF SOURDOUGH WHEAT BREAD, 300G FARMHOUSE LOW-FAT FROMAGE BLANC, BUTTER (OPTIONAL).

FOR THE TOPPING: 4 SPRING ONIONS (SCALLIONS), FINELY CHOPPED, 10 RADISHES, THINLY SLICED, GUÉRANDE GREY SALT, FRESHLY GROUND BLACK PEPPER.

This tartine is certainly the one which inspired me to create these open sandwiches. One of the places where it is traditionally served is the Marolles district, the most authentic and typical of the 'real' Brussels, close to the local flea market. Early in the morning, antique dealers and second-hand goods traders can be seen seated at tables, enjoying it with a draught beer.

- Spread the fromage blanc on the slices of bread, which may be buttered according to taste. Cut each slice into 5 triangles. Arrange on the sandwich boards. To garnish each board, opt for touches of colour and freshness, such as a melon quarter, a few slices of cucumber with the skin, a sprig of dill or of flat-leaved parsley.

- Farmhouse fromage blanc, which still goes by the name of "maquée" in Belgium, can be replaced by ricotta from Italy or "brousse de brebis" (a very soft sheep's milk cheese) from France. If necessary, it may be strained through a sieve or muslin an hour in advance, then kept chilled.

Raw beef, Parmesan shavings, virgin olive oil and basil tartine

FOR **4** PORTIONS:

4 LARGE SLICES OF SOURDOUGH WHEAT BREAD, FRESH BUTTER, 300G ULTRA-FRESH FILLET OF BEEF (BOUGHT THAT DAY), MEDIUM-GRAINED GREY SEA SALT, FRESHLY GROUND BLACK PEPPER, 4 TBSP EXTRA VIRGIN OLIVE OIL, 10-12 FRESH BASIL LEAVES, 80G PARMIGIANO REGGIANO CHEESE, SHAVED.

FOR THE TOPPING: SUN-DRIED TOMATO MARINATED IN OLIVE OIL, OLIVES, ROCKET LEAVES, LEMON. IN SEASON, SLIGHTLY UNDER-RIPE FRESH TOMATO, I.E. JUST TURNING RED OR EVEN SLIGHTLY GREEN.

Apart from fillet, lean pieces of leg of beef can be used. A slice of entrecôte (rib) steak, trimmed of the fat and membranes, is also delicious.

The Parmesan can be shaved using a potato peeler, a truffle grater or a cheese spade.

- Slice the beef with a sharp knife. Use a flat knife or a spatula to spread the chilled raw beef onto the buttered bread, pressing down on it so that it adheres to the slices of bread. Season with salt and pepper.
- Roughly chop the basil and mix it into the olive oil. Spread this mixture onto the meat. Then sprinkle over the Parmesan shavings. Trim the crusts at the far left and right ends of each slice of bread and cut it into 5 neat triangles.
- Finally, garnish with the rocket leaves, tomato quarters, olives and lemon.

Ham-butter tartine

The thickness of the slices of ham gives a special flavour, different from that of thin slices, something which is probably down to the 'chew'.

Under national organic legislation in Belgium the use of nitrite salts is prohibited. This 'Organic Ardennes' ham is therefore cured using only unrefined Atlantic sea salt. L'Impériale mustard, made by a long-established Belgian company, is that of my childhood. The secret recipe produces a pure and natural mustard containing no artificial colours or preservatives. It is milder than Dijon mustard.

In this recipe, Dijon or even Savora mustard (also made in France) can be substituted for L'Impériale variety.

FOR 4 PORTIONS:
4 LARGE SLICES OF SOURDOUGH WHEAT BREAD, FRESH BUTTER, 4-5 THICK (5-6MM) SLICES OF ORGANIC COOKED HAM.
FOR THE TOPPING: ORGANIC MUSTARD À L'ANCIENNE (OLD-FASHIONED STYLE), NIÇOISE-STYLE OLIVE MUSTARD, L'IMPÉRIALE MUSTARD, A FEW GHERKINS.
FOR THE NIÇOISE-STYLE OLIVE MUSTARD: 50G DIJON MUSTARD, 50G BLACK OLIVE PASTE.

- To make the niçoise-style olive mustard, mix together the mustard and the olive paste in a bowl with a fork.
- Divide out the ham on the buttered slices of bread and cut each slice into 5 triangles. Arrange on the sandwich boards. Serve with gherkins and the assortment of three varieties of mustard.

Brie de Meaux and walnut tartine

This tartine has been on Le Pain Quotidien's menu since the very beginning. It is incredibly simple but a true classic which never goes out of fashion. Good quality farmhouse Camembert can be substituted for Brie.

FOR **4** PORTIONS:
4 LARGE SLICES OF SOURDOUGH WHEAT BREAD, 1 250G TRIANGULAR PIECE OF RAW MILK BRIE DE MEAUX CHEESE RIGHT FOR EATING, 50G OF TOP QUALITY, FRESH SHELLED GRENOBLE WALNUTS.
FOR THE GARNISH: RADISHES, CUCUMBER.

- Thinly slice the brie and spread it on the bread, top with the walnuts, pressing so that they adhere to the cheese. cut the sandwiches into triangles, arrange on the boards and garnish.

5 vaches qui rient tartine
for kids from 1 to 101 years old

FOR **4** PORTIONS:
4 SLICES OF SOURDOUGH WHEAT BREAD, 20 TRIANGLES ORGANIC PLAIN CHEESE SPREAD, OR ALTERNATIVELY PLAIN LA VACHE QUI RIT BRAND (LAUGHING CAW) CHEESE SPREAD, 20G RAW GREEN PISTACHIOS, COARSELY CHOPPED, 10G BROWN SESAME SEEDS OR LINSEEDS, 4 TSP CHIVES, CHOPPED, PINCH OF CATALAN MILD SMOKED CHILLI POWDER.

- Cut each slice of bread into 5 triangles. Carefully remove the triangles of cheese from the foil without squashing them. Soak the top side in the different ingredients. Arrange on the bread.

Beef tartare à l'ancienne (old-fashioned style) tartine

FOR **4 PORTIONS:**

4 LARGE SLICES OF SOURDOUGH BREAD

FOR THE TARTARE: 250G LEAN BEEF (SIRLOIN OR RUMP STEAK) , 2 TSP ORGANIC MUSTARD À L'ANCIENNE (OLD-FASHIONED STYLE), 2 TSP WORCESTERSHIRE SAUCE, 1 TBSP SALTED-CURED CAPERS, 1 TBSP ONION, CHOPPED, 1 TBSP PARSLEY, CHOPPED, PEPPER, DASH OF TABASCO, 4 TBSP EXTRA VIRGIN OLIVE OIL, 1/4 TSP SALT.

FOR THE TOPPING: PICKLED GHERKINS, CHOPPED PARSLEY, POIVRE MIGNONNETTE (COARSELY GROUND BLACK PEPPERCORNS), FINELY SLICED ONION.

This tartare can also be served on toasted bread, provided that the bread is removed from the toaster and left to cool for a few minutes.

Tartare 'purists' are free to add a raw egg yolk to this preparation if they so wish.

- Take the beef out of the refrigerator just before slicing it. The beef needs to be cold, as this makes it easier to cut. Using a very sharp knife, cut it into 6mm thick slices. Cut them into 6mm wide slices. Finally cube the slices.
- In a well chilled large bowl, mix the meat in with the other ingredients using a fork until all the other ingredients are well combined.
- Spread the mixture onto the bread and draw lines lengthwise using a fork. Cut into triangles and arrange on sandwich boards.
- Serve with crunchy gherkins and the onion, parsley, pepper and caper garnish.

Pot-boiled curried chicken salad
with date and harissa chutney tartine

FOR 4 PORTIONS:

4 LARGE SLICES OF SOURDOUGH WHEAT BREAD, FRESH BUTTER.

FOR THE CURRIED CHICKEN SALAD: 300G CHICKEN COOKED IN VEGETABLE STOCK, 100G FULL-FAT FROMAGE BLANC OR THICK SOUR CREAM, 100G MAYONNAISE, A PINCH OF MADRAS CURRY POWDER, SALT, 40G ONIONS, CUT INTO SMALL CUBES, 40G CELERY, CUT INTO SMALL CUBES, 1 TSP WHITE WINE VINEGAR.

FOR THE DATE AND HARISSA CHUTNEY: 100G DATES, STONED (PITTED), 5CL HOT WATER, 1 TSP WINE VINEGAR, 1 TSP HARISSA, PINCH OF SALT.

FOR THE TOPPING: A PINCH OF DILL OR CHOPPED CHIVES, A FEW SLICES OF RIPE MANGO, DICED TOMATOES, CRISPY GHERKINS, LETTUCE LEAVES.

Cooking a chicken in stock means that the fat can be skimmed off and is thus one of the best ways of obtaining very lean poultry meat. This tartine is one of the most elegant solutions to use up left-overs.

- Marinate the diced celery, with a pinch of salt and a teaspoon of white wine vinegar, for 12 hours.
- For the chutney, marinate the dates with the vinegar and water for 10 minutes, add the salt and harissa. Pestle them in a mortar to obtain a smoothish paste. An alternative is to use a fork to crush the ingredients in a flat bowl or a soup plate.
- Mix together the fromage blanc, mayonnaise, curry and salt with a fork in a bowl. Blend in the chicken, onion and drained celery.
- Spread the mixture onto the slices of bread, added the diced tomatoes and cut each slice into 5 triangles. Arrange on the sandwich board. Garnish with slices of mango, lettuce, dill, chives and small gherkins.

At that stage (early 1995), I no longer owned Le Pain Quotidien as such. My story had been too good to be true and so it lasted for only a little over four years.

As is the case when any business expands too quickly, I had had cash flow problems. To illustrate the problem, we were making a profit of €140,000 by the end of the second tax year, 14 months after selling the very first sandwich.

But that sum was exactly the amount of our liabilities. And we needed to invest, without being able to touch these liquid assets, which were spoken for. The banks had granted me a leasing arrangement and two loans, on unfavourable terms. If I wanted more credit, I had to produce balance sheets for three years, which was obviously an impossibility. So the banks refused to back me any further. Another problem was that I was behind with payment of my social security contributions, which are very high in Belgium. The Ministry had sent bailiffs, who had started noting everything down – ovens, kneading machine, shelves, etc. I thought to myself that Le Pain Quotidien had just two months to turn itself around, before it became insolvent, a state of affairs brought about by pressure from the Belgian government authorities.

But investors in the sector were interested in Le Pain Quotidien. Michel Montignac was one of them. He was at the peak of his fame. Millions of copies of his books on losing weight the healthy way were being sold. He came to Belgium to open a Montignac store, for which he needed bread supplies. I met him and we made bread for him for a time. He would have liked to take things further, either to buy me out or to go into partnership with me.

I was coming under pressure from all sides so decided to approach the Van de Kerkhove group. Although this large family-owned business operated on an industrial scale, I was impressed by its professionalism and the quality of its management. I had bought bread from them at Le Café du Dôme. They baked excellent baguettes. I had visited one of their plants, which was brand new, and I liked the fact that they employed real pastry cooks, who still worked by hand.

The Van de Kerkhove family naturally left me to stew in my own juice. They needed time to study the situation, which, incidentally, allowed them to 'rescue' me in the nick of time, just before the scheduled bankruptcy. They laid down their conditions and bought 60% of the stock of my company, SA Le Pain Quotidien, whilst also requesting me to buy out the holdings of my two original partners. The agreement also stipulated that Van de Kerkhove had an option on the remainder of my share of the company!

That clause was valid for the next five years. But they exercised their option after just one year. So in late 1994, I sold my remaining 40% holding in the company. I was leaving the business which I had set up four years earlier and which I had nurtured and seen expand, thus giving up both the production unit and the two stores which I owned, including the very first one on rue Dansaert.

I still had a little money left and, even more importantly, the ownership of the brands, which I had registered in my own name. This had been negotiated in exchange for a little more money and the right to exploit Le Pain Quotidien licence in three markets: the USA, France and Japan. I immediately lodged a licence application, setting up a company especially for that purpose, called PQ Licensing SA, which still exists to this day. But that's another story...

Tuna, tapenade and grilled sweet pepper tartine

FOR 4 PORTIONS:

4 LARGE SLICES OF SOURDOUGH BREAD, 200G TUNA IN BRINE, 1 EGG YOLK, 1 TSP MUSTARD, SALT, PEPPER, A DASH OF LEMON JUICE, 6 TBSP EXTRA VIRGIN OLIVE OIL, 1/2 CUP CELERY AND ONION, DICED, PARSLEY, CHOPPED.

FOR THE TOPPING: 3 TBSP BLACK OLIVE PASTE, 1 SMALL RED SWEET PEPPER, FRESH HERBS, MIXED SALAD, LEMON QUARTERS, 12 BLACK OLIVES, 4 THIN SLICES OF SUN-DRIED TOMATOES.

- Carefully strain the contents of the can of tuna through a sieve.
- Roast the whole red pepper over a gas burner (or on a barbecue) for 5 minutes. Skin it and cut it into strips.
- Blend the egg yolk, the mustard, the lemon juice and olive oil with a small whisk. Add the salt and pepper, onion, pepper and parsley.
- Finally add the crumbled tuna. Mix carefully. Adjust the seasoning if necessary. Spread the mixture onto the sandwiches. Dilute the olive paste with a drop of lukewarm water to make it more fluid.
- Draw a line of olive paste on the sandwich, cut into triangles and garnish with the strips of grilled sweet pepper.
- Arrange on the sandwich boards and decorate with lemon, black olives, sun-dried tomatoes and herbs.

Another way of removing the pepper skins easily is to roast them in an oven at 200°C for 10-15 minutes. Wrap them up in a plastic bag for a few minutes, then peel them.

Tuna, green herb purée and capers tartine

FOR 4 PORTIONS:

4 LARGE SLICES OF SOURDOUGH WHEAT BREAD, 20G FRESH BUTTER, 250G DRAINED TUNA, 2-3 TBSP SALT-CURED CAPERS, SALT AND PEPPER.

FOR THE HERB PURÉE: 5G SALT, 150ML EXTRA VIRGIN OLIVE OIL, 100G MIXED GREEN HERBS (AS AVAILABLE: FLAT-LEAVED PARSLEY, BASIL, SPINACH, CHIVES, TARRAGON, SORREL), 1 EGG YOLK, 1 TBSP MUSTARD, WORCESTERSHIRE SAUCE.

FOR THE GARNISH: DICED TOMATOES, GHERKINS, OLIVES, SUN-DRIED TOMATOES, ROCKET.

If you wish, you can make a larger amount of green herb sauce. The combined action of the olive oil and the salt means that it will easily keep in the refrigerator for several days if protected by plastic film. It can also be frozen. It is a perfect accompaniment for grilled sardines or grilled meat, and even poached poultry.

- To make the green herb purée, blend the herbs with the salt and oil in an electric blender until a fine purée has been formed. Stop the blender and add the egg yolk, the mustard and a dash of Worcestershire sauce.
- Mash the tuna with a fork, add the crushed capers and 100g of green herb purée. Season with salt and peper. Mix quickly so as not to form too smooth a mixture, spread on the slices of buttered bread decorated with a few diced tomatoes.
- Cut each slice into 5 triangles and arrange on the sandwich boards.
- Serve with several condiments – gherkins, olives, sun-dried tomatoes, a few rocket leaves.

Red kidney bean and harissa cream hummus tartine

FOR 4 PORTIONS:

4 LARGE SLICES OF SOURDOUGH BREAD, FRESH HERBS.

FOR THE HUMMUS: 200G FRESHLY COOKED OR CANNED RED KIDNEY BEANS,
1 TBSP FRESH CORIANDER, 2 TBSP SPRING ONIONS (SCALLIONS), CHOPPED,
1/2 GARLIC CLOVE, CHOPPED, JUICE OF 1/2 LEMON, 2 TBSP EXTRA VIRGIN OLIVE OIL, SALT.

FOR THE HARISSA CREAM: 2 TBSP HARISSA, 75G TAHINI, PINCH OF SALT, 75G WATER.

FOR THE DECORATION: 1 TBSP PARSLEY, CHOPPED, 50G TOMATOES, DICED, THIN SLICES
OF LEMON.

Black beans or cooked chickpeas can be used in this recipe. If you cook them from scratch, be sure to soak the black beans or chickpeas for the recommended time beforehand and only add salt to the cooking water at the very end.

- For the hummus, mix the beans roughly with the crushed garlic, lemon juice, olive oil and salt. Add the coriander and the spring onions at the last minute. The traditional recipe for hummus can be followed and the beans finely puréed to produce a smooth paste.

- For the harissa cream, whisk all the ingredients together for 20 seconds until an emulsion forms. Spread the hummus on the bread cut into triangles. Sprinkle with parsley (or other fresh herbs) and add diced tomato and thin slices of lemon.
- Spoon the harissa cream onto the sandwich board, decorating it with a line of plain harissa.

Egg salad, extra virgin olive oil, wild capers and anchovies tartine

FOR 4 PORTIONS:

4 LARGE SLICES OF SOURDOUGH BREAD, BUTTERED. 6 HARDBOILED FARM EGGS,
6 TBSP EXTRA VIRGIN OLIVE OIL, 1 TSP MUSTARD, 1/2 CUP CHOPPED HERBS
(1/3 PARSLEY, 1/3 SPRING ONION (SCALLION), 1/3 DILL), 6 TWISTS BLACK PEPPER.

FOR THE TOPPING: 50 SMALL SALT-CURED CAPERS, 10 FLAT FILLETS OF ANCHOVY
IN OLIVE OIL.

FOR THE DECORATION: 4 TOMATO QUARTERS,
4 MELON QUARTERS, GHERKINS, BUNCHE OF HERBS.

- Slice the hardboiled eggs thinly with an egg slicer (guitar type), turn 90° and slice them a second time to produce a julienne.
- Place the mustard, olive oil and black pepper in a bowl, beat with a small whip, add the julienne of eggs and the chopped herbs.
- Mix for 10 seconds, taking care not to 'purée' the eggs. Spread the salad on the buttered slices of bread, divide out the capers and cut each slice into 5 triangles. Arrange on the sandwich boards and garnish each triangle with 2 anchovy fillets.
- Decorate with tomato quarters and melon, gherkins and a bunch of fresh herbs.
- Basil or chervil can also be used in the mix of herbs.

Avocado, nori and spring onion (scallion) tartine

Nori is a red alga (seaweed) belonging to the Porphyra species which is traditionally used in several countries. The world champion Nori eaters are the Japanese, who have popularized it worldwide in the form of the paper-thin crispy sheets used as wrapping for sushi. Traditionally it is recommended that they be toasted on a flame before they are eaten.

The avocadoes need to be ripe but firm. Take them out of the refrigerator just before peeling.

FOR 4 PORTIONS:

4 LARGE SLICES OF SOURDOUGH BREAD, 3 RIPE AVOCADOES, 2 TBSP LEMON JUICE, SALT, TABASCO.

FOR THE TOPPING: 1 TOMATO, WITH THE SEEDS REMOVED AND CUT INTO DICES, 4 TBSP CHOPPED BULBS OF THE SPRING ONIONS (SCALLIONS), 1/2 CUP JULIENNE OF NORI, 8 NORI TRIANGLES (BASE: 6CM), LEMON QUARTERS, SLICES OF CUCUMBER AND RADISH, SPRIGS OF DILL AND FLAT-LEAVED PARSLEY, 1 WHOLE AVOCADO.

- Place three peeled avocadoes with the salt, Tabasco to taste and a dash of lemon juice in a large bowl. Mash roughly with a fork.
- Spread this mixture onto the slices of bread. Sprinkle with the diced tomato and the chopped stalks of the spring onions. Cut the slices of bread into 5 regular triangles. Sprinkle with the julienne of seaweed. Arrange on the sandwich boards, decorate each sandwich with 1/4 fanned avocado, 1/4 lemon, slices of cucumber and radish, 2 triangles of nori and the bunch of herbs.

Peanut butter and miso sauce tartine

FOR 4 PORTIONS:

4 LARGE SLICES OF SOURDOUGH BREAD, 10G BLACK SESAME SEEDS, 10G BROWN SESAME SEEDS, 10G FLAX SEEDS, 10G SUNFLOWER SEEDS, 10G PUMPKIN SEEDS, 1 SHEET OF NORI SEAWEED.

FOR THE PEANUT CREAM: 100G PEANUT BUTTER, 50G WATER, 50G MISO SAUCE (SEE RECIPE P.190).

- Place the three ingredients of the peanut cream in a bowl and whip vigorously until a thin emulsion forms. Spread the sauce onto the slices of bread. Sprinkle the different seeds on top and cut each slice into 5 triangles. Arrange them on the sandwich boards and sprinkle them with a julienne of Nori seaweed.

Tartare of vegetables and tahini cream tartine

This tartare can be served as a salad with toasted bread. Smoked salmon or prawns (shrimps) can also be added.

Tahini is an oily paste made from ground and roasted sesame seeds (hulled or unhulled).

FOR 4 PORTIONS:

4 LARGE SLICES OF ORGANIC SOURDOUGH WHEAT BREAD, LIME OR LEMON.

FOR THE TAHINI CREAM: 100G TAHINI, 100G SPRING WATER, PINCH OF SALT.

FOR THE TARTARE OF VEGETABLES: 50G JULIENNE OF CARROTS, 50G TOMATOES, DICED, 1 TBSP OF THE GREEN PART OF SPRING ONIONS (SCALLIONS), CHOPPED, 50G RED CABBAGE, GRATED, 50G GREEN LENTILS, GERMINATED FOR 3 DAYS, 1/4 GARLIC CLOVE, 50G JULIENNE OF CELERIAC, 1/2 AVOCADO, 2 TBSP FLAT-LEAVED PARSLEY, CHOPPED, WORCESTERSHIRE SAUCE, 1 TBSP CAPERS, 3 TBSP OLIVE OIL, JUICE OF ONE LEMON, DIJON MUSTARD, SALT, PEPPER.

FOR THE TAHINI CREAM

- Blend all the ingredients for 20 seconds to produce an emulsion of the oil in the water. The same physical principle as a mayonnaise is involved.

FOR THE TARTARE OF VEGETABLES

- Chop each of them finely to produce a julienne, using a vegetable mill or a mandoline.
- Place all the ingredients in a large bowl so that they can be mixed together thoroughly. Spread the slices of bread with the tahini cream. Spread the tartare of vegetables on top. Cut each sandwich into 5 triangles. Arrange on a serving dish or individual sandwich boards and serve with quarters of lime or lemon.

6

Flour and oil

Seen from abroad, it appears fairly logical for a Belgium-based chain to sell chocolate. So from the day when the rue Dansaert store opened, 'Charlemagne' brand small chocolate squares were sold at the counter.

'Charlemagne' brand chocolate and I go back a long way. I knew the company's founders, Jean-François & Denise Stas, when they were starting out in business.

I had spotted their 100g chocolate bars in an organic food store. They were stacked in boxes and not individually wrapped. There was only one variety: the chocolate contained crystallized sugar and was cinnamon-flavoured, making it distinctive.

For Le Café du Dôme, I was looking for small individual portions of chocolate of the kind served at the end of a meal, with tea or coffee.

As I wanted something different from the regular brands, I went to see Jean-François at his farm near Liège. At the time he was still a farmer and produced bars of chocolate because it was his hobby, something about which he was passionate. He sold them on markets and through organic food networks. He was not equipped to produce individual sizes, even less to wrap them.

At the time, I had met Jean Galler, who has since made a name for himself in the world of chocolate. Amongst other things, Jean marketed small 7g or 8g chocolate squares, which he sold in bars and cafés. If I remember rightly there were two 'flavours': plain dark chocolate and milk chocolate. He was not prepared to customize production for me and certainly not to copy Jean-François Stas. On the other hand, he lent Jean-François some moulds and agreed to personalize the Charlemagne square wrapping for Le Café du Dôme. He charged me two cents per ten units for this service.

Taking advantage of the opportunity which I had given them, Charlemagne extended their range to include other flavours. I seem to remember that the marketing of their first square boxes of 24 chocolates coincided with the opening of the first Le Pain Quotidien bakery and store.

It was a similar story with my flour supplier, the milling group Cérès. When I first started out, I received 50kg sacks of flour. With the move to the rue de la Poudrière premises and, even more importantly, the increase in the number of stores in Belgium, we shifted into high gear. Cérès installed a storage silo for me and I paid it off on credit. But I was aware that the stone-ground flour supplied by Cérès was not the best available. And some of my customers, local good food gurus, had no hesitation in telling me that Poilâne bread was better than mine and that its ingredients were of better quality.

So I went back to Lionel Poilâne's supplier, Decollogne-Lecocq millers, who were based in the Seine-et-Marne département not far from Paris. Apart from the obvious quality of their production, these millers were already known at the time for their organic flour. I asked them to supply me with it because 'going organic' was an ideal that I was already pursuing at the time. But they were unwilling to sell it to me. Thinking back, it was probably because they had too little of it in the early 1990s.

So we agreed on 'regular' flour and the delivery comings and goings started. It didn't last long. First of all, the logistics proved difficult to manage. They supplied 5-6 tonnes of flour in bulk twice a week, using a small truck. To make the 300 kilometre trip between Précy-sur-Marne and Brussels cost-effective, they added one or two pallets of sacks at the rear of the vehicle. The exercise was clearly a major challenge for them. In fact there were occasions when I ran out of flour for a few hours.

Another thing was that my Belgian millers, Cérès, very soon realized that I was going behind their backs and obtaining bread flour elsewhere, even though I was still obtaining supplies of flour for pastries, croissants, etc., from them. Cérès pointed out in passing that the silo belonged to them. My response was that I was not satisfied with their flour.

So we made a joint technical visit to Decollogne-Lecocq mills. Cérès then asked me for a sack of the flour that I used. Two months later, their technicians came back with samples of really fantastic quality flour. In the meantime, they had changed their technology and adapted the grinding stones, so that they could now offer me the quality I was seeking at a far more reasonable price. We worked on that basis until Le Pain Quotidien went organic. Their flour supplied Le Pain Quotidien outlets in the USA for a long time.

It was in spring 1993 that I met the Mahjoub family. The four brothers and seven sisters all lived in the centre of Tebourba, an agricultural locality in the Medjerda valley, around thirty kilometres from Tunis. They were and still are landowners and farmers. In addition, they own a magnificent oil mill – of which they are justifiably proud – in the centre of their small town.

At the time, major changes were occurring in Tunisia. During his 'reign', Habib Bourguiba had nationalized the market in most of the country's key products, such as cereals, olive oil, cork and wine.

His successor, President Ben Ali, embarked on liberalization of the economy, allowing the bosses of companies in the sector to market and export their products. Majid Mahjoub, the third of the brothers, was thoroughly familiar with the subject. At the time, he was a close associate of the Minister for Planning, having worked as an economist at the National Oil Office.

He and his three brothers had only one dream, which was to follow in the footsteps of their father who, in his time, used to travel to France to sell the fruits of his labour, in the form of a particularly famous and well regarded extra virgin olive oil.

His two older brothers, Salah, the man of the soil, and Abdel, the intellectual, both studied in Belgium and were keen on the idea of exporting to Brussels, the capital of Europe.

That was how they came into contact, via the Belgian development cooperation office in Tunis, with one of my close friends, an agricultural engineer, who was then the husband of the designer of Le Pain Quotidien logo.

The Mahjoub brothers had commissioned him to help them to export their olive oil by giving it a commercial image. Two months after his first trip to Tebourba, this friend and I took a plane together. And I discovered for myself what he had told me about with such enthusiasm: a traditional oil mill with hydraulic presses dating back hundreds of years and still producing first and second cold-pressed olive oil. Almost no one still works like that nowadays as the equipment required has simply not been kept.

The oil produced during the previous marketing 'year' – from mid-December 1992 to late February 1993 – was stored in tanks and venerable wooden casks. Raouf, the youngest brother and the manager of the oil mill, gave me my first tasting of extra virgin olive oil straight from the barrel.

Salah, the head of the family, the man who worked the land, the farmer, then took us on a tour of the estate, in his capacity as a landowner. We went up to the highest point on the farm, a small protuberance in the landscape where the Romans had already built an oil mill. It was magnificent! No need to add that the crops were grown ecologically, with a love verging on the religious of the nourishing earth.

Salah was also the manager of a local agricultural cooperative which processed the olives and produced mixed vegetables. His expertise was remarkable. His small niçoise olives and the green olives with fennel and candied lemon – which he nicknamed "olives cassées" – were quite simply sublime. As these products were not subject to the same administrative control as oil, he could export them and even supplied them to the Jewish community in Paris. His Tunisian olives were therefore kosher and certified as such by a rabbi.

On each of our visits, we invariably stayed at the family home, a square-shaped house in which the number of bedrooms remains a mystery, as I never managed to figure out exactly how many there were. Mrs Mahjoub always prepared the first meal for us, family dishes about which I am convinced there must have been something symbolic. Her daughters then took over. It was an extraordinary sight to see them arriving in the evening, dressed in the traditional white shawl, carrying at arm's length the hot dishes which they had spent a good part of the day preparing in their kitchen.

I'll spare you the details of all the varieties of couscous and tajines which the Mahjoub sisters prepared for us in turn over those three or four days and on the occasion of each of our subsequent trips – but I can assure you that they were all delicious.

I have particular memories of the kitchen where we ate breakfast, dipping toasted bread into soup bowls full of extra virgin olive oil. It was at the same oilcloth-covered table that we discussed prices and packaging. My agricultural engineer friend had decided that the oil should be positioned as a top-end product. The visual identity of the future labels was ready. It was then that I suggested using the typical Burgundy wine half-bottle (37cl capacity). The brand image of Les Moulins Mahjoub had been created and I was to place my first order for a few hundred litres, supplemented by an assortment of mixed vegetables and olives. It was much later on that other products were added, such as the sea salt-cured wild capers which the family prepared for its personal consumption.

There are some ventures on which it is better to embark without knowing all the ins and outs in advance. Otherwise, you would give up, which would inevitably be the wrong thing to do.

This particular venture comes into that category. Because purchasing products is one thing. Ensuring that they arrive safe and sound, which means putting up with the administrative formalities and trying to cut through the red tape, is quite another.

At the time, Europe was still protecting its internal market by applying quotas, levying import taxes on certain products, including olive oil. So I went through the long, hard battle of going from one department to the next to pay a guarantee, then returning several times until the official responsible for issuing the appropriate form happened to be in the office.

But by fall 1993, I was able to display on the shelves of Le Pain Quotidien stores extra virgin olive oil which I had selected and of which I was the sole distributor. It was something of a long shot at a time when everyone swore by Italian oils from Tuscany, and people were not slow to point this fact out to me.

My reply was that I could offer total traceability, a direct line between producer and consumer. Another point was that cutting out the middlemen enabled me to have affordable prices and to use Mahjoub products in cooking. Whether it is oil, wine or bread, when you want to sell food or drink, you need to take customers into your confidence, so to speak, so that they understand exactly what you are offering them.

You come to realize that with sufficient charisma, people respect your approach and follow the trend you have set. And Le Pain Quotidien had already become something of a guru in this area. This 'phenomenon' was confirmed later, with sun-dried tomatoes.

I discovered them in a small Italian restaurant, a place atypical of Brussels, which I liked a lot and where I first ate mozzarella di buffala, which arrived on a direct flight from Naples twice a week.

L'Ombra was what I call a 'non-restaurant', by which I mean a house converted into a restaurant. There was no furniture for serving the food, no cash register, no arrow indicating the bathroom.

You had the impression that you were eating in someone's home.

The decor included large glass jars of sun-dried tomatoes in oil, in which large salt-cured capers floated. As I thought they were really good I started buying the sun-dried tomatoes through the owner of L'Ombra. They were used in cooking. Our growth and the rocketing number of stores also caused supply difficulties here and we sometimes ran out. Then the day came when we were asked to wait for the next harvest. Because the tomatoes had to be planted, grown, sun-dried, etc.

In addition, as my restaurateur's margins were comfortable, our stores operating under franchise were finding the bill too steep. I tried to obtain sun-dried tomatoes direct from southern Italy, but I failed to find the product that I wanted. Firstly, most are packed in sunflower oil. Secondly, to extend shelf life and to preserve the bright red colour, citric acid is generally added, and that was something I definitely didn't want.

That was how I came to think of the Mahjoub family's farm. They had no experience of tomato growing or of sun drying but they wanted to extend their range. For the first harvest, they called on Sicilian agricultural technicians. For the drying process, they referred to age-old sun-drying techniques, which they use in particular for M'hamsa, a traditional variety of couscous.

Thus it was that in the intense heat of early July in Tunisia, I found myself on the roofs of the farm, where Salah and I dried the first tomatoes.

When the first jars arrived in Brussels, the sun-dried tomatoes were far too salty!

There is a straightforward explanation as to why this happened. To start the drying process, the tomatoes have to be halved, then sprinkled with salt. This has two effects. Firstly, to absorb the vegetation water and to act as a pump. Secondly, as in many cases of this kind, to protect the product by means of a sort of natural bacteriostatic barrier. We had clearly gone over the top, our logic being consistent with 'He who can do more can do less', as the saying goes.

Even so, we managed to find buyers for our first jars of sun-dried tomatoes in extra virgin olive oil and salt! But I have to admit that we used a lot of them in the dishes on our menu – which at least had the advantage of making savings on salt!

The next harvest of sun-dried tomatoes in olive oil was absolutely top quality. They were so neatly stacked in the jars that they looked almost as if they were 'laminated'!

When the tomato drying process had been mastered, Majid Mahjoub suggested olive paste. I had asked him if he could supply me with a tapenade but there had been a problem with mechanization of pitting of the small niçoise olives. They resolved it and their olive paste has become a pure olive purée, with a little oil. In the USA, several magazines have adopted it as their current favourite 'dip'!

Majid is always looking for new ideas. One day he asks you to taste artichoke hearts in oil. Their consistency and flavour are unique, thanks in part to the use of real freshly squeezed lemon juice. Another day he comes up with a sun-dried garlic purée in oil.

But Tebourba harissa is one of his most magical products. He has succeeded in giving this traditional Tunisian condiment an exceptional flavour, attributable no doubt to the way in which the chillies are roasted, giving them a slightly smoky taste.

Succeeding in putting some of the flavours and smells of one's native soil into a glass jar is probably the secret of happiness – although talent obviously plays a large part too. Up there, Salah, who left this earth far too soon to join the stars of all the nights he worked, must be looking down and smiling.

Toasted tartine and millefeuille of vegetables

FOR **4** PORTIONS:

4 LARGE SLICES OF TOASTED SOURDOUGH WHEAT BREAD, GREEK YOGURT, FRESH MINT, FRESH CORIANDER, PAPRIKA, TOMATO.

FOR THE MILLEFEUILLE OF VEGETABLES: | MEDIUM AUBERGINE (EGGPLANT), | COURGETTE (ZUCCHINI), | SMALL WHITE ONION, | GARLIC CLOVE, FRESH THYME AND ROSEMARY, SALT, PEPPER, 6 TBSP EXTRA VIRGIN OLIVE OIL, 75G PARMESAN, GRATED OR VERY FINELY SHAVED, OR EWES' MILK FETA.

The millefeuille of vegetables can be prepared the day before and reheated either on the bread under the grill, or in a microwave oven.

In the Middle East, labneh, a yogurt from which the whey has been removed by straining, is commonly available. On the same principle the Greek yogurt can be strained through a conical strainer an hour before use.

- Finely slice the vegetables using a mandoline. Arrange half the courgettes, oil, thyme, garlic, salt and pepper in an earthenware dish (15cm x 25cm). Place half the onions, aubergines, salt, pepper, rosemary and cheese on top. Repeat the operation so that there are four layers in all.
- Bake in a conventional oven at 175°C for 30 minutes or place in a microwave oven, covered with a plate, and cook for 2 minutes three times in succession.
- Cut the millefeuille of vegetables into four portions and place them on the toasted bread cut into 4 pieces. Serve with a Greek yogurt with fresh mint and coriander sauce, with a dash of smoked paprika for added spice.
- Decorate each piece with a very thin slice of slightly under-ripe raw tomato to add a touch of freshness.

Chickpea with rosemary, roasted garlic and tapenade bruschetta

This dish, ideal for summer drinks parties at the pool side, can be served at room temperature. It can even be prepared in advance and then returned to the oven briefly before serving.

The freshly toasted slices of bread can also be rubbed with a raw garlic clove.

The thickness of the slice is of fundamental importance if a toasted open sandwich, which is what an Italian bruschetta is generally taken to mean, is to hold together properly. A thick slice makes for a soft centre and a crunchy crust. In addition, if the filling is juicy, a thicker slice absorbs the liquid better. That is the reason why at Le Pain Quotidien we do not toast slices which are 11mm thick.

FOR 4 PORTIONS:

3-4 LARGE SLICES OF SOURDOUGH WHEAT BREAD, 15MM THICK, 6 GARLIC CLOVES, THINLY SLICED, 2 TBSP BLACK OLIVE PASTE, 1 TSP HARISSA, SALT, 3 TBSP EXTRA VIRGIN OLIVE OIL, 1 SPRIG FRESH ROSEMARY, 300G FRESHLY COOKED OR CANNED CHICKPEAS, 1 BAY LEAF, 1 TBSP BALSAMIC OR RED WINE VINEGAR, 1 TBSP PARSLEY, CHOPPED.

- Soak 100g of chickpeas in water overnight. Drain, rinse and cook them in unsalted water with a bay leaf for 11/2 hours. Alternatively open a can of cooked chickpeas.
- Fry the garlic and rosemary gently in the olive oil in a non-stick frying pan or wok for one minute. Add the chickpeas, the tapenade and the harissa and fry the mixture gently for 2-3 minutes. Deglaze with the vinegar, season with the salt to taste and add the parsley.
- Spread the chickpea mixture onto the bruschetta and serve immediately.

Sardine, beetroot and lime bruschetta

FOR **4 PORTIONS:**

3-4 LARGE SLICES OF SOURDOUGH WHEAT BREAD, 15MM THICK, SLICED WITH A KNIFE,
2 CANS SARDINES IN OLIVE OIL, 1 BEETROOT, 2 LIMES, 1 TBSP FRESH CORIANDER, CHOPPED,
SALT, PEPPER, 1 TBSP VIRGIN OLIVE OIL, 1 GARLIC CLOVE.

- Lightly toast the slices of bread and rub them with a raw garlic clove, according to taste. Cut them into pieces.
- Open the cans of sardines and remove them carefully, taking care not to break them. Set aside on a plate. Grate the beetroot into a fine julienne. Season with the juice of 1/2 a lime, salt, freshly ground pepper, the olive oil and the chopped coriander. Mix together well.
- Arrange this salad on the pieces of bread, add one sardine per slice and serve with quarters of lime separately.

Wild green asparagus and
al pepe nero Pecorino bruschetta

FOR 4 PORTIONS:

3-4 LARGE SLICES OF SOURDOUGH WHEAT BREAD, 15MM THICK, SLICED WITH A KNIFE,
150G WILD ASPARAGUS SPEARS (OR, ALTERNATIVELY, VERY FINE GREEN ASPARAGUS SPEARS),
1 TOMATO, 125G BLACK PEPPER PECORINO, EXTRA VIRGIN OIL, SALT.

Small raw globe artichoke hearts or raw button mushrooms cut into thin slices can be substituted for asparagus in this recipe.

Plain Pecorino or Parmesan with plenty of freshly ground pepper can be substituted for black pepper Pecorino. But it would be a pity not to use this wonderfully flavoursome variety of cheese.

- Wash the asparagus and cut the spears to 5-6 cm in length. Split them in half lengthwise, put them into a bowl and season with salt and olive oil. Cut the tomato in half, deseed it, then cut it into strips. Preheat the grill by lighting it or switching it on at the maximum position. Cut the slices of bread into rectangular pieces, toast both sides under the grill. Cut them into pieces.
- Spread the asparagus salad onto the pieces of bread, finely shave the Pecorino over the asparagus using a truffle mandoline or a potato peeler. Place the garnished pieces of bread under the grill as near as possible to the source of heat and allow the cheese to melt for 30 seconds, until it colours slightly. Remove from the grill and garnish with the strips of tomato. Add a few drops of olive oil.
- Serve piping hot.

Salt cold ceviche bruschetta

FOR 4 PORTIONS:

3-4 LARGE SLICES OF SOURDOUGH WHEAT BREAD, 15MM THICK, SLICED WITH A KNIFE,
200G COEUR DE FILET (CENTRE CUT) SALT COD, 1/2 RIPE AVOCADO, DICED, 2 RADISHES,
CUT INTO A FINE JULIENNE, LIME (OR LEMON).

FOR THE MARINADE: 1 LIME, 1 FIRM TOMATO, 1/2 CRUSHED GARLIC CLOVE,
1 SPRING ONION (SCALLION), FINELY CHOPPED, 2 TBSP MIXED CHOPPED HERBS
(PARSLEY, CORIANDER, DILL, SMALL AMOUNT OF MINT), SALT, 1/4-1/8 JALAPEÑO
(SMALL GREEN CHILLI PEPPER), FINELY CHOPPED (QUANTITY DEPENDING ON HOW HOT IT IS).

If salt cod is not available, several other firm fresh fish can be used, examples being monkfish, cod and sea bass. Other possibilities are scallops, giant shrimps and lobster – or even a mixture of them all. Naturally, all these fish are to be used raw.

This is a wonderful recipe to go with Tequila- or vodka-based cocktails.

- Soak the salt cold in water in the refrigerator overnight to remove the salt.
- Peel the lime. Dice it, using a sharp knife. Skin and dice the tomato.
- Mix these two ingredients with all the other ingredients in the marinade.
- Using a large sharpened knife, cut the fish into thin strips and place them in a wide dish with all the marinade ingredients. Mix carefully and marinate in the freezer for 5 minutes.
- Lightly toast the slices of bread and cut them into pieces.
  Place the marinated fish on the toasted pieces of bread. Add the thinly sliced radish and the avocado cubes.
- Serve garnished with pieces of lime or lemon.

Hazelnut flûte and Gorgonzola

This is an ideal combination of bread, nuts, raisins and cheese. It goes down a treat with a glass of white wine, made from "Vendange Tardive" (late harvest) grapes if possible...so likely to be from Alsace.

FOR 4 PORTIONS:

4 GRILLED HAZELNUT AND RAISIN FLÛTES (SMALL AND THIN FRENCH STICKS), 250G GORGONZOLA.

- Halve each flûte sideways. Quickly grill each inner surface. Spread on 3-4mm of gorgonzola.

Pain d'épices and carpaccio of duck foie gras tartine

To make it easier to cut the foie gras neatly, plunge the blade of the knife into very hot water.

It is important to choose a make of "pain d'épices" containing very little sugar. The optimum thickness of the slices is 7-8mm. Thin slices of toasted sourdough wheat bread may also be used.

FOR 4 PORTIONS:
8 THIN SLICES OF PAIN D'ÉPICES (VARIETY OF GINGERBREAD NOT TOO SWEET), 160G OF VERY FRESH CHILLED RAW DUCK FOIE GRAS CRU, GUÉRANDE GREY SALT, FRESHLY GROUND BLACK PEPPER.

- Use a very thin and sharp-bladed knife to cut the foie gras into slivers. Place them on the slices of pain d'épices. Cut the slices into triangles. Season with the coarse salt and coarsely ground black pepper. Serve immediately as this dish is best eaten well chilled.

Seared foie gras and cep (porcini) bruschetta

FOR 4 PORTIONS:
3 LARGE SLICES OF SOURDOUGH WHEAT BREAD, 15MM THICK, SLICED WITH A KNIFE, 240G LOBE OF RAW DUCK OR GOOSE FOIE GRAS, 200G FRESH CEPS (PORCINI), WASHED AND TRIMMED, SALT, PEPPER, 1 TBSP EXTRA VIRGIN OLIVE OIL, 1 TBSP SHALLOTS, CHOPPED, 1 TBSP CHIVES, CHOPPED.

- Sauté the washed and trimmed mushrooms in the olive oil, adding the chopped shallot just before the mushrooms are cooked. Season with salt and pepper. Set aside and keep warm. Preheat the grill by lighting it or switching it on at the maximum position. Cut the slices of bread into rectangular pieces, toast both sides under the grill. Cut the foie gras into 1cm thick slices. Place them on the bread under the grill as near as possible to the source of heat and sear the foie gras for 20-30 seconds. Remove from the grill and garnish the pieces of bruschetta with the pan-fried ceps. Season with coarse salt, freshly ground black pepper and chopped chives. Serve immediately.

Whole cereal bread, smoked salmon and strained yogurt tartine

This preparation can be given slightly more 'bite' by adding 1-2 teaspoons of strong to medium mustard to the strained cheese. Mix well.

Full-fat yogurt can also be used in this recipe, as can soya (soy) milk yogurt.

I prefer mild smoked salmon because it is not too salty. Other smoked fish, such as eel, trout, swordfish and even canned smoked cod liver in oil, go well with whole cereal bread.

SERVES 4:

8 THIN (6-7 MM) SLICES OF WHOLE CEREAL BREAD (WITH OR WITHOUT GLUTEN), 4-6 SLICES MILD SMOKED SALMON, 2 LOW-FAT NATURAL YOGURTS OR 250G FAT-FREE FROMAGE BLANC.

FOR THE DECORATION: DILL OR CHIVES, PEPPER.

- In the morning, pour the yogurt or fromage blanc into a coffee filter and leave to strain over a bowl in a cool place (refrigerator or cold cellar) for at least three hours.
- Spread the strained yogurt onto the bread. Garnish with smoked salmon, cut into thin strips. Add the dill or the chopped chives. Serve with freshly ground black pepper.

Whole cereal bread, pear slices, stilton and traditionally made pear syrup tartine

"Sirop de Liège" is traditionally produced in eastern Belgium, in a dairy farming region. In days gone by, the meadows, the main feature of this hedged farmland landscape, were full of apple trees and, especially, pear trees with long-stalked leaves. Whereas other regions convert overproduction into cider or spirits (Calvados), a syrupy apple and pear concentrate has been produced here for generations, to store for the winter. According to tradition, the syrup is made by reducing whole fruit, cooked in large copper cauldrons over wood fires, for hours on end. Production units of this kind are now very rare. And it is to be feared that some new set of regulations issued by European bureaucrats will put an end to this gastronomic tradition. Yet another one!

Traditional "sirop de Liège" contains only fruit sugar. Its deep, warm flavour is a perfect match for its amber colour. It can be stored at room temperature for several years without spoiling.

SERVES 4:

8 THIN (6-7 MM) SLICES OF WHOLE CEREAL BREAD (WITH OR WITHOUT GLUTEN),

2-3 PEARS (CONFERENCE OR COMICE), JUST RIPE, 200-250G FARMHOUSE STILTON CHEESE,

4 TSP TRADITIONALLY MADE SIROP DE LIÈGE.

FOR THE SEASONING (OPTIONAL): FRESHLY GROUND BLACK PEPPER, JALAPEÑO

- Quarter the pear without peeling it. Remove the pips (seeds) and cut into thin strips.
- Arrange them on the bread, thinly spread with "sirop de Liège" beforehand. Add shavings of Stilton.
- Freshly ground black pepper or jalapeño can be added as seasoning.

Manhattan

The setting up of Le Pain Quotidien in New York started with my meeting a man called Bob Scarborough. It happened in 1994. Bob was living in Belgium at the time. He was manager of a small American company based in Ghent. He and his wife Lisa were planning to open a Le Pain Quotidien outlet in the USA. At almost the same time I got a similar request, this time from a Belgian who had done business in the anchovy canning sector in Morocco. Given the sheer size of the American market, I put them in touch with one another. They discovered that their respective wives sang in the same choir in Brussels on Sundays.

In the end, I awarded the master franchise for the East Coast to this composite tandem. One of the clauses in our contract provided for the formation of a company, each partner, myself included, contributing seed money of $100,000 so that the pilot store could be opened. Today I realize just how stupid I was. I didn't think of demanding a set-up charge. I thus entrusted one of the largest potential markets to two individuals who would quite simply pay 1% royalties on the sales of the first store and bakery and 2% subsequently, starting from the second store.

A few months later I arrived in New York. First of all we needed a good location. Appointments with realtors were made. It should be pointed out here that in the meantime, the two potential partners had fallen out in a big way. The Belgian partner had pulled out and never reappeared on the scene. This was two years before the opening of 1131 Madison Avenue.

Things got off to a good start. We found a 140 m2 commercial property, with a basement level, which was well situated, at the level of 85th Street, The commercial lease was signed in spring 1995 and the owner gave us four months rent-free. As things turned out, four months would be far from long enough because the first American Le Pain Quotidien only opened on January 12 1997!

In the end, we were to pay a monthly rent of €14,500 for 15 months for nothing. The bill came to €220,000 before we were able even to sell a single sandwich! In fact, the signing of this lease marked the start of a long, hard battle, which was to lead to my being based in New York for several years.

Apart from a few round trips, at the time I was living in Brussels, where my Belgian business activities took up all my time and energy. First and foremost, there was Le Pain Quotidien, of which there were now upwards of fifteen branches. I also got involved in a number of other business ventures, with mixed results, such as a tapas bar and a restaurant right next to the first store in rue Dansaert, which had been called La femme du boulanger .

I also opened a restaurant in partnership with Eric Bosschman, a brilliant sommelier. We had planned a counter selling bread. We kept to the biblical theme in choosing the name. It was – and still is – called Le Pain et le Vin (Bread and Wine).

Across the Atlantic, the Madison Avenue opening had stalled. When the lease had been signed we had ordered the furniture from the Belgian manufacturer who was the official supplier to Le Pain Quotidien. The furniture arrived in New York and was stored in the future outlet, pending its opening, which was now hypo-thetical. Bob told me that the banks had refused him the loan for which he had applied. So I became his backer, to the point where the money which I had managed to save ran out. But I had no choice. Because the store's opening had become more than vital. As the building work progressed, Bob Scarborough had constantly sought extra funding, at a rate of $50,000 a month. If the worst were to happen and Le Pain Quotidien didn't open, I would find myself penniless, back to square one, in almost the same situation as when I had first arrived in New York as a private chef, 13 years earlier. Such a failure would also mean that there would be virtu-ally no hope of expansion in the American market – and for several years at that. And it should be remembered that in the meantime I had lost control of the business in Belgium.

Before managing to open the New York store we also made some monumental errors.

The story of the bread oven is a textbook case, 'what not to do' in a nutshell, a model of absurdity to be studied by business school students. We ordered the oven at the same time as the furniture. The oven, dispatched by the German supplier who had fitted out the first Belgian bakery, arrived in New York by air. It was in a packing case measuring 3 metres by 6 metres. It proved impossible to get the fully assembled oven inside the box into the Madison Avenue basement because of the height of the ceiling. So it was stored somewhere in the Bronx for two years. Later, when we opened the SoHo store, we had it moved by crane but soon realized that it was oversized there too. So it was never actually used. Add the $15,000 Bronx warehouse rental to the $300,000 purchase price and a few other costs. That makes a lot of tied up capital for a penniless new company and all for an oven which in the end had to be disposed of by selling it off at half price.

So I bought different ovens, modular electric ones, which were in fact better suited to baking pizza rather than bread. I was able to use them to bake cakes and pastries, croissants, baguettes and rolls. For the 2kg round sourdough loaves, I made a deal with Amy Schreiber of the Amy's Bread bakery. I supplied her with the bread pans and the stone-ground flour, imported from Belgium. During the final stage of the work on the Madison Avenue premises, I grew the first fresh sourdough culture in the cellar, while training Amy's baker in the use of natural sourdough starter, without regular baker's yeast.

At the time, I was based permanently in New York, to ensure that the work on the store was finally completed. I rented a room for $230 a week at the Pioneer Hotel, 341 Broome Street, very close to

Little Italy and Chinatown. Reputed to be the oldest hotel in NYC, it's the sort of place where backpackers stay overnight, with rooms just 3 metres long and 1.50 metre wide. With the bed wedged against the wall, there's just 5 cm left for baggage. The toilets and showers (all shared) are in the corridor. It's not possible to stay at the Pioneer for more than a month at a time. It's the hotel's way of protecting itself, as after a month a client can become resident at that address, meaning that he/she would be virtually impossible to evict. So every month I stayed elsewhere for 48 hours, then went back to the Pioneer.

I stayed there until one of my friends from Brussels came to help me out, in the run-up to the opening. He's very much a party animal and made so much noise that we got thrown out. So I ended up sleeping on a mattress at 1131 Madison Avenue.

Finishing off the refurbishment work was very much an amateur affair. In turn, I nailed down the floor, plastered the walls and put a coat of paint on the cellar walls.

We opened at 7 am on Saturday January 12 1997. There was no cash left to buy an espresso machine. At the eleventh hour the Lavazza distributor loaned us one, in exchange for which we had to serve his brand of coffee.

The only place with running water was a wash bowl, in which someone washed the dishes in cold water and without any detergent. The plumber worked all day and most of the night, so that on the Sunday morning we had hot water. And an operating dishwasher!

Pierre Mendrowski and Frédéric Nicolay, from Le Pain et le Vin restaurant, came over from Brussels to help me. Their support was more than welcome. We didn't sleep a wink for 72 hours. Because our 140 m2 store at 1131 Madison Avenue very quickly became a success.

This was all down to the fact that a 'good fairy' had happened to pass by on January 10. Her name was Florence Fabricant. On the Thursday, she had found herself in that part of Madison Avenue by chance and had seen the enamelled sheet metal sign 'Le Pain Quotidien – Bakery & Cafe', which had already been nailed to the façade. From the outside, she didn't know what to think of this new store, because large sheets of paper had been stuck onto the windows. So she went in and asked the electrician a few questions, while I was perched on a ladder, painting the ceiling.

I can't remember whether I got down from the ladder but I can still see her asking whether we had already contacted the New York Magazine. Naturally, we hadn't had the time to think about details like that.

It was then that she introduced herself and explained that she was a gossip columnist on the New York Times, more specifically the gastronomy column. And we were clearly set to form part of the small circle of gourmet eateries. She asked us not to contact any rival journalist for two weeks and not to give any interviews.

On the Friday evening, a photographer from the New York Times turned up at the shop. It was 8 pm, the first loaves had arrived. We just had time to put the pots of jam, jelly and spreads, the chocolates, the olive oil, etc., into the display cupboards. The following Wednesday, a quarter-page feature appeared in the New York Times, with the photo and Florence Fabricant's article. At the time the quarter-page spread seemed more like double that amount of coverage to me!

It took around a month to reach cruising speed. While our sales on the first Saturday totalled $1700, four or five weeks later our Saturday takings had reached $7000. Today we make double that figure or more.

Once the store was open I went home to Belgium, thinking that the hardest part was over and that everyone would manage just fine. I had no plans whatsoever to live in the USA.

Bob Scarborough was a nice guy, who was very welcoming and very good with our customers. But he very quickly proved to be an ineffectual manager. In fact it took me three or four months to find out what was going on.

The situation was paradoxical. On the one hand, this first US Le Pain Quotidien outlet was doing very well and sales were rising steadily. On the other, Bob was still asking me for extra funding, even though just getting the store open had cost me a phenomenal €700,000, a sum of money which I obviously did not have, meaning that I had had to find a new Belgian partner.

The point is that the setting up of small businesses is lightly regulated in the USA. No lawyers are involved. The subscription of capital is more or less informal. It is not subject to specific checks, nor is the depositing of the funds.

So there was no way that I could get involved and find out what was happening, especially as Bob Scarborough was the founder and sole official administrator of the company, as well as being chairman of the board. I couldn't consult the accounts either.

Once you have some business experience, you realize what's wrong. In the case in point, we were stuck between a rock and a hard place, between two conflicting realities. On the one hand, our wage costs were too high, while on the other, our prices had proved to be too low in relation to our 'competitors'. Having sorted this out, I got involved in the production side and the kitchen, where the employees considered me to be the real boss. Then I put pressure on the accountant, simply to find out what was going on, because I did not have access to the accounts, namely a clear statement of the daily cash flow situation. The upshot was that the accountant resigned.

So I took a look at the figures and discovered to my horror that the bank account was in disarray. Even worse, it was patently obvious that Bob Scarborough had never invested a penny in the business, not even his initial $100,000 stake. We were literally on the verge of bankruptcy.

To put all this into perspective, a few years on from that debacle, the Madison Avenue store now has annual sales in excess of $3 million. In eight years we have gone from one to twelve stores. We continue to obtain our supplies as far as possible in Europe, by the container load. Initially, containers arrived every four or five months. Now jam, chocolate, crockery, furniture, etc., cross the Atlantic every ten days.

Beyond these figures and the aura that our presence in New York gave us in Europe (an outlet opened in Paris a few months later), we were able to enjoy the fruits of our labours, the sort of thing that cannot be felt anywhere else in the world, not on that scale at any rate.

In our microcosm, that of food, great chefs are hugely important, especially as in the USA they have megastar status. Several of the famous names, so-called uber-chefs, came in turn to Le Pain Quotidien as customers. They spend the whole year with ingredients such as caviar, foie gras and truffles, so they appreciate simplicity for what it is, if it manages to hit the right note. If it is overdone, it is no longer simple. If not enough is done, anyone can copy it.

Jean-Georges Vongerichten often comes to the SoHo branch of Le Pain Quotidien with his family on Sundays. We also supply two of his restaurants, Jean Georges and Mercer Kitchen.

Daniel Boulud, one of my friends, came shortly after the opening. Alfred Portale, with whom I had worked at Michel Guérard's restaurant en 1983, was one of our first loyal customers. He asked us to supply bread to his Gotham Bar & Grill, the famous restaurant on 12th Street, not far from Fifth Avenue. Later, Alain Ducasse made the same request for his chic bistro, Mix, in New York.

Manhattan offers such a concentration of all kinds of celebrities that some of them are bound to come to your store. For instance, I was introduced to Martha Stewart, the American lifestyle guru, not to say goddess. She owned an apartment near the Madison Avenue store, on the Upper East Side. She came in just like that, incognito. Everyone seemed to know her. As I never watched American TV, I had no idea who I was talking to.

In late 1998, she did something really wonderful for us. She and her team really liked the atmosphere of the large communal table. A week before Christmas, before everyone went away, she organized her 'business' Christmas party on our premises. It was a select gathering for the media elite, the bosses of the leading television channels and of magazines

We closed the Madison Avenue store at 4 pm. There was no kitchen as such, only the bakery, but I prepared veal flanks. They were left to cook gently for hours on baking trays in the bread oven. As an appetizer there were blinis with Hoegaarden white beer, which were also cooked in the oven. Martha Stewart had brought the caviar and the dessert, an ice cream layer cake which we served with our 'home-made' tarts.

She had liked the meal as the following year – in late 1999 – she invited me on to her TV show. And together we reproduced the bakery's Christmas menu. She had recreated Le Pain Quotidien atmosphere in the studio, with the large table, the pine furniture, etc.

She remained loyal to the extent that on the day her company Martha Stewart Living Omnimedia Inc. was to be floated on the stock exchange, she asked us to provide breakfast. She had set up a marquee on Wall Street. When all the stock exchange dealers and traders arrived for work at 8 am, she gave them a small basket containing Le Pain Quotidien croissants and pains au chocolat, fresh orange juice, an individual portion of butter, etc.

I delivered all this, enough to feed in excess of 1500 people, in the middle of the night, right opposite the New York Stock Exchange.

Garlic and bread soup

Keep stale dry bread in a metal tin, taking care to ensure that it is moisture-free. This can be done by putting it on a plate and leaving it overnight on a radiator. Two weeks later, when the tin contains a variety of different types of bread (rye, spelt, sour-dough wheat, etc.), it is time to put a good home-made soup on the menu.

The same types of bread, turned into crumbs in a food processor, also produce excellent home-made breadcrumb coating.

SERVES 4:

200G STALE BREAD, 8 GARLIC CLOVES, 2 TBSP PARSLEY, ROUGHLY CHOPPED, 1.5 LITRES WATER OR CHICKEN STOCK, 1/2 TSP SALT.

FOR THE ACCOMPANIMENT: EXTRA VIRGIN OLIVE OIL, PECORINO OR PARMIGIANO REGGIANO.

- Heat up the water, the bread, cut into cubes or sticks, the salt and the quartered garlic cloves in a 3-litre pot. Bring to the boil, turn down the heat and simmer for 15 minutes.
- Remove from the heat and add the parsley. Serve accompanied by good quality olive oil.
- A chunk of Pecorino or Parmigiano reggiano and a truffle grater can also be placed on the table, so that cheese shavings can be sprinkled onto the soup.

One-minute sun-dried tomato and bulgur wheat soup

The twofold action of the sun and salt means that halved tomatoes, from which most of the seeds have been removed, will become desiccated.

It takes 13-14kg of fresh tomatoes to produce 1kg of the sun-dried variety. Their flavour is very different from that of fresh tomatoes, being much more pronounced, more rustic, with a preserved, almost spiced tang.

SERVES 4:

100G SUN-DRIED TOMATOES IN OLIVE OIL, 2 GARLIC CLOVES, 75G BULGUR WHEAT, 30G CELERY, 1 SPRIG THYME, 1 BAY LEAF, 2-3 TBSP EXTRA VIRGIN OLIVE OIL, 2 TBSP FRESH BASIL, CHOPPED, 1.25 LITRES WATER, 1/2 TSP SALT.

- Bring the water to the boil with the salt, thyme and bay leaf. Slice the sun-dried tomatoes into a fine julienne. Chop the garlic and the celery.
- Add the bulgur wheat to the pot and allow to boil for one minute. Remove from the heat, add the basil and olive oil and serve immediately.

Barley soup and PGI Ardennes ham

This soup tastes better with a twist of freshly ground pepper. Black pepper or a mix of several peppers are best.

PGI (protected geographical indication) Ardennes ham is a raw ham produced by combining a limited number of operations: salting, which involves rubbing dry salt into the pig's thigh, the stage preceding actual curing, during which the future ham loses a proportion of its water content. The hams are then hung and left to mature in a cold atmosphere, reminiscent of winter, then washed to lower the salt content. The final stage is smoking of the hams.

SERVES 4:

160G PEARL BARLEY, 2 GARLIC CLOVES, CHOPPED, 100G ONIONS, 100G CELERY, 100G LEEKS, 100G CARROTS, 1 SPRIG THYME, 1 BAY LEAF, 1 CLOVE, 2 LITRES WATER, 1 SMALL TSP SALT.

FOR THE GARNISH: 2 TBSP CHIVES, CHOPPED, 1 TBSP LIGHTLY SALTED FARMHOUSE BUTTER, 4 SLICES ARDENNE HAM, CUT INTO A FINE JULIENNE.

- Peel the onions and carrots. Trim the leeks. Cut them and the celery into 1cm cubes.
- Put all the ingredients into a pot with the lid on, then simmer gently for an hour and a half.
- When cooked, add the ham in julienne and leave to rest over a very gentle heat for 5 minutes.
- Just before serving, add the fresh butter and chives and serve immediately.

White bean soup and rocket (arugula) vinaigrette

Canned – ready-cooked – beans are ideal for this recipe and cut preparation time considerably. If you prefer to use dried beans, you will need 100g, cooked for two hours in unsalted water. Remember that you need to soak them beforehand in three times their volume of water, for at least 12 hours.

SERVES 4:

400G COOKED WHITE BEANS, 1 SPRIG THYME, 1 BAY LEAF, 1 LARGE CARROT, DICED, 1 CELERY STICK, DICED, 2 GARLIC CLOVES, CHOPPED, 1.5 LITRES WATER, 1/2 TSP SALT.

FOR THE GARNISH: 2 HANDFULS WASHED AND DRAINED ROCKET, 3 TBSP EXTRA VIRGIN OLIVE OIL, 1 TBSP RED WINE VINEGAR, SALT, PEPPER.

- Boil the water with all the soup ingredients for 20 minutes. Remove the sprig of thyme and the bay leave. Remove a quarter of the volume and blend. Return to the pot with the unblended soup. Adjust the seasoning by adding salt to taste.
- In a salad bowl, add the vinaigrette to the rocket. Serve the bowls of soup immediately, garnishing with a handful of rocket salad.

Maman Mahjoub potato and "olives cassées" soup

SERVES 4:

300G WAXY POTATOES, 15 OLIVES VERTES CASSÉES (LEMON FENNEL OLIVES), 2 GARLIC CLOVES, CHOPPED, 1 SMALL ONION, CHOPPED (75 G), 1/2 TSP DRIED CUMIN, 1 SPRIG THYME, 1 BAY LEAF, 1 PINCH OF LEMON PEEL, 1 LITRE WATER, 1/2 TSP SALT.

TO FINISH OFF: 2 TBSP EXTRA VIRGIN OLIVE OIL, 2 TBSP PARSLEY, CHOPPED.

- Peel the potatoes and cut them into 1-2cm dice.
- Put all the ingredients into a 3-litre pot. Bring to the boil and simmer for 25 minutes. Turn off the heat and add the chopped parsley and olive oil at the last minute.

Brussels sprouts with cheese soup

In the north of France, "extra-vieux Mimolette" cheese is ready to eat after being left to mature for 11-14 months. It is an orange-coloured cows' milk cheese, its trademark colour traditionally coming from carrot juice, which is also used to colour Cheddar and Double Gloucester. However, Mimolette is harder in consistency, allowing it to be grated. In Holland, the other Mimolette country, it is called "Commissie kaas".

Cheddar and other similar cheeses can be substituted for Mimolette in this recipe.

SERVES 4:

300G FRESH BRUSSELS SPROUTS, PINCH OF NUTMEG, 20G BUTTER, 1 ONION, 1 SPRIG THYME, 1-2 GARLIC CLOVES, 150G POTATOES, 50G GRATED EXTRA-VIEUX MIMOLETTE CHEESE, 1.25 LITRES WATER, 10G SALT, PEPPER.

FOR THE GARNISH: 60G EXTRA-VIEUX MIMOLETTE CHEESE.

- In a non-stick frying pan, sauté in the butter over a high heat for 5 minutes the quartered Brussels sprouts, the chopped onion, the thinly sliced garlic, the thyme and the finely cubed potatoes. When they have turned colour slightly, transfer to a 3-litre pot. Add the water and salt and simmer for 10 minutes.
- Pour half the soup into the blender bowl. Add the grated fresh nutmeg and 50g of Mimolette cheese.
- Blend well, pour onto the rest of the soup and adjust the seasoning (salt and freshly ground pepper).
- Serve immediately, accompanied by a bowl of grated or shaved Mimolette cheese.

Puy green lentils with Lapsang Souchong tea soup

Instead of a tea bag, 3g of Lapsang Souchong tea leaves, finely crushed in a mortar, can be used.

Lapsang Souchong is a smoky tea from Fujian province in China. Immediately after picking, its leaves are 'withered' over a fire of pine and cedar tree branches. This black tea is not widely drunk in China, being mainly an export product. Its smoky, woody flavour, evocative of liquorice, lingers in the mouth, leaving behind a hint of bitterness. It is a sophisticated and subtle tea which is low in theine/tannin and is ideal to drink with a salty meal.

SERVES 4:

150G PUY GREEN LENTILS, 100G ONIONS, 100G CARROTS, 100G CELERY, 2 GARLIC CLOVES, 1 SPRIG THYME, 1 BAY LEAF, 200G TOMATOES, 1 LAPSANG SOUCHONG TEA BAG, 2 TBSP VIRGIN COLZA OIL OR EXTRA VIRGIN OLIVE OIL, 1.25 LITRES WATER, 1/2 TSP SALT.

FOR THE GARNISH: 2 TBSP PARSLEY, CHOPPED.

- Sweat the oil, onions, carrots, celery and quartered garlic with the thyme and the bay leaf in a pot.
- After five minutes, deglaze with the water, add the lentils and the Lapsang Souchong tea, bring to the boil and simmer for 40 minutes. Remove the tea bag. Add the unpeeled cubed tomatoes and the salt, cook for a further 5 minutes, adding the parsley at the last minute.

Beetroot (beet) and red cabbage Bortsch

SERVES 4:

200G RAW RED BEET(ROOT), 150G RED CABBAGE, 100G ONIONS, 60G CELERY, 60G CARROTS, 2 GARLIC CLOVES, CHOPPED, 1 SPRIG THYME, 1 BAY LEAF, 1 CLOVE, 2 JUNIPER BERRIES, 125G POTATOES, 8 BLACK PEPPERCORNS, 1.5 LITRES WATER, 1/2 TSP SALT.

TO FINISH OFF: 1 TBSP WINE VINEGAR , 1 CUP SPRING (GREEN) ONIONS, CHOPPED, 125G SOUR CREAM OR STRAINED YOGHURT, 1/2 CAN TOMATOES, CUBED (APPROXIMATELY 200G).

The sour cream can be replaced by full-fat fromage blanc or strained yogurt. To strain the yogurt, simply put it in a paper coffee filter and refrigerate for two hours. Use 300g of low-fat or full-fat yogurt, i.e. three individual pots..

- Roughly cube all the vegetables and put them into the pot with the water and the other ingredients. Bring to the boil and simmer gently, with the lid on, for 30 minutes.
- Add the vinegar and the canned tomatoes. Cook for a further 2-3 minutes. Adjust the seasoning by adding salt to taste and serve with the thick sour cream and the spring onions.
- The fact that Bortsch needs to be cooked for a comparatively long time means that the liquid may evaporate considerably.
- If it tastes too concentrated, you can add a little boiling water just before serving, in which case adjust the seasoning.

Oat soup with kitchen garden herbs

SERVES 4:

125G ROLLED OAT FLAKES, 1 GARLIC CLOVE, 50G PARSLEY, 50G CHERVIL, 50G SPINACH, 25G BASIL, 3 TBSP EXTRA VIRGIN OLIVE OIL OR VIRGIN COLZA OIL, 1.5 LITRES WATER, 10G SALT.

The mixture of green herbs can be varied at will, using fresh thyme, rocket, lettuce, raw broccoli and young radish tops, to name but a few.

The same proportions of barley, quinoa or rice flakes can be substituted for oats.

- Wash the herbs and spinach thoroughly. Remove most of the stalks, so that 50g net (drained and dried) of each remains.
- Put the water, oat flakes, salt and chopped garlic into a pot, bring to the boil and simmer over a low heat for 5 minutes. Remove a quarter of the oat soup and pour into the blender bowl with the herbs and the oil. Blend for 1-2 minutes until the mixture is creamy and smooth.
- Serve the white oat soup in soup bowls and pour the green soup into the middle. Serve immediately.

Two days later he sent us a leaflet with full details of the building. I returned a week later to meet the owner of the property. We negotiated the lease, which was signed on February 1. We commissioned an architect, ordered the oven, the furniture and everything else. We opened on July 22 2001, just six months later.

Although this appears quick compared with the Madison Avenue experience, a great deal of time was in fact wasted. Planning regulations are very strict in Beverly Hills. It is not possible to choose the colour of the façade or signs, even the most innocuous being regulated. Since the 1994 earthquake, all buildings have had to be strengthened, especially at roof level. All furniture has to be attached and cupboards have to be anchored into walls. To open four small windows on the side, three engineers had to be consulted.

Carrying out a construction project in Beverly Hills is a nightmare. No truck can be unloaded before 10 pm. We were even forced to empty the container with the furniture during the night. When we opened, we brought one of our bakers – a guy from Senegal – over from New York to lend our French baker a hand. We had rented a small apartment for him, five or six blocks from the store. So at midnight he had to walk let's say a kilometre to go and bake the bread. He only did it once. On the second night, a whole lot of police cars turned up. The cops jumped him, pinned him to the ground and handcuffed him. It would appear that it's not normal for a black man to walk around on his own at night in Beverly Hills. He was so traumatized by the experience that he asked to go back to New York immediately.

Besides this, Los Angeles being the movie capital, we are spoilt for choice when it comes to stars of all kinds. When Christophe Lambert comes to Le Pain Quotidien, he goes and has a word with the bakers to tell them the bread is great. But the star who is really fond of us is Jamie Lee Curtis. She lives in Santa Monica, but her office is located alongside the Beverly Hills branch of Le Pain Quotidien. She comes in at around 9 or 10 am. She adores our granola and even praises it in her interviews.

She's very approachable. One day when we were looking at the plans for the future store in Brentwood with the architects, she came over and asked where we were thinking of opening, suggesting other good locations.

Brentwood opened in March 2002, followed by Melrose in late June. Three stores in eleven months! Two were also opened in New York that year. Five openings in a year is a huge financial undertaking when you don't happen to have a millionaire grandmother.

Los Angeles gave us a different perception of America. New York is a very international city. Consumers are sophisticated, akin to European gourmets. In California, people come to Le Pain Quotidien more for the decor and the atmosphere than for the food.

Of course, there are microcosms, like Brentwood, the 'street mall' of the people who live on the hill. When they get into their cars, it's the first place where they can find a few stores, where they can buy a pack of cigarettes, find a photo development lab, a hairdresser, a dry cleaner's, a little Italian restaurant where they can eat a quick snack. All actors are very much at ease in Brentwood, because buses with hordes of tourists don't descend on it. The day of the opening, Brooke Shields came twice, very cool in her little red jeep. The second time she realized that I was not American and spoke to me in perfect French. Dustin Hoffman also buys his bread there. He is very much into good food. I believe that he was also one of the Brentwood store's very first customers.

Sprouted Puy green lentils, red cabbage and Feta cheese salad

Puy green lentils are an "appellation d'origine contrôlée" (AOC) – registered designation of origin – product, grown in a volcanic area at the heart of the Haute-Loire département, on the Velay high plateaux (altitude: 600-1200m). They are grown without fertilizers or irrigation.

These lentils contain minerals (iron, magnesium), amino acids, trace elements and proteins and their fat content is very low.

To make them more digestible, the sunflower seeds can be soaked in spring water for around 24 hours. Soaking them removes their transparent outer skin.

SERVES 4:

75G PUY GREEN LENTILS, SPRING WATER, 1/4 RED CABBAGE (APPROXIMATELY 300G), SALT, FRESHLY GROUND PEPPER, 2 TBSP VIRGIN COLZA OIL, 2 TBSP RED OR WHITE WINE VINEGAR, 1 TBSP SUNFLOWER SEEDS, HULLED, A LITTLE GARLIC, CHOPPED (OPTIONAL), 100G EWES' MILK FETA.

- Four days before, start germinating the lentils. Rinse in cold water, drain, put in a large bowl and cover with water. Soak for 24 hours at room temperature. The next day, remove the lentils from the water, rinse and drain through a sieve.
- Put the sieve on a bowl, leave uncovered at kitchen temperature for three days. The ideal temperature is 20°C. If it is cooler, germination may take an extra day.
- Repeat the rinsing and draining operation every 12 hours. After three days the lentils will have germinated, each with a sprout measuring 1/2-1 cm.
- Finely chop the cabbage with a mandoline or a knife.
- Put it in a large bowl and add the sprouted lentils, the sunflower seeds, the vinegar, oil, garlic (optional), salt and pepper. Arrange on plates, adding 25g cubed Feta to each plate.

Seaweed and miso sauce salad

There are dozens of different types of miso in Japan. In outline, rice, barley or soya (soy) are cooked and fermented with koji (a yeast also used to brew sake). The traditional method involves fermentation in casks and takes months, if not years.

Used by the Japanese for thousands of years and in Celtic countries since at least the Middle Ages, seaweed is generally sold dried. The most common varieties include dulse, wakam, sea lettuce, arame and iziki.

SERVES 4:

25G DRIED MIXED SEAWEED, SPRING WATER.

FOR THE MISO SAUCE: 25G MISO PASTE, 75G WINE VINEGAR, 1 TSP VIRGIN ROASTED SESAME OIL, 100G SOYA (SOY) SAUCE, 50G SOYA (SOY) OIL, 50G WATER, 1 TSP WHITE OF EGG, 25G LEMON JUICE.

FOR THE GARNISH: CUCUMBER, RADISH, SPRIGS OF DILL, 1 LEMON, 1 TBSP TOASTED SESAME SEEDS.

- Soak the seaweed in 1/2 litre of cold water for 30 minutes, then drain.
- Place all the miso sauce ingredients in a bowl and blend for 20 seconds to form an emulsion.
- Arrange the seaweed salad in a dome in the middle of four plates and surround each dome with 4 thin slices of cucumber, 4 thin slices of radish, a sprig of dill and a lemon quarter.
- Sprinkle with sesame seads. Serve the sauce separately.

Mint and lemon taboulé

SERVES 4:

50G FINE BULGUR WHEAT (OR MEDIUM-GRAINED COUSCOUS), 1 CUP FLAT-LEAVED PARSLEY, CHOPPED, 10 MINT LEAVES, CHOPPED, 1 LARGE TOMATO, SLIGHTLY UNDER-RIPE, 1/2 TSP CUMIN, 10 TWISTS FRESHLY GROUND PEPPER, 1 PINCH GUÉRANDE FINE GREY SALT, JUICE OF ONE LEMON, 1 CUP CUCUMBER JULIENNE, 4 TBSP EXTRA VIRGIN OLIVE OIL.

FOR THE GARNISH: TOMATOES, MELON, WATERMELON, CUCUMBER, MINT LEAVES, PARSLEY, BASIL, CORIANDER OLIVES, LEMON, EXTRA VIRGIN OLIVE OIL.

- Cut the tomato into cubes with the skin and seeds. Thinly slice the cucumber with the skin and seeds, then cut into strips to form a julienne.
- Put all the ingredients, except the lemon, into a large bowl and chill in the deep-freezer for 10 minutes or in the refrigerator for an hour.
- Take out the well chilled bowl and the lemon juice. Mix thoroughly. Mould the taboulé in a small bowl or a cup which has been coated with olive oil. Turn out in the middle of four large plates.
- Garnish with seasonal products arranged around the moulded taboulé: 3 thin tomato quarters, 3 melon or watermelon triangles, thin slices of cucumber, a few large mint leaves, olives, 1 lemon quarter, fresh herbs (parsley, basil, coriander, etc.)
- Serve with a good quality extra virgin olive oil on the table.

Bulgur is generally made from hard (durum) wheat. This is cooked in water, then dried to harden the inside. It is moistened again, which strengthens its outer skin. At this stage it is roughly milled, removing the bran and the germ. Prepared in this way, bulgur has a long shelf life.

Quinoa with grilled aubergines (eggplant) and lemon salad

Quinoa, a plant revered by and sacred to the Incas, originates in the Altiplano in the Andes and is reputed to be the world's most nutritional cereal. Protein-rich, its grain contains all the essential amino acids, including arginin and histidin, which are essential for babies. Another remarkable feature of this Chenopodiacea is that it is gluten-free.

Quinoa comes in the form of flakes, which can be used in soups or sweet milk-based desserts. The flakes are delicious cooked in soya (soy) milk, to which honey or fresh fruit can be added.

SERVES 4:

200G QUINOA, 2 MEDIUM AUBERGINES (EGGPLANTS), 2 RIPE TOMATOES, 1 SMALL BUNCH FRESH BASIL (OR CORIANDER OR PARSLEY), 1 PINCH SALT AND FRESHLY GROUND PEPPER, JUICE OF ONE LEMON, 4 TBSP EXTRA VIRGIN OLIVE OIL OR VIRGIN COLZA OIL.

FOR THE GARNISH: EWES' MILK FETA CHEESE.

- Cook the quinoa in 4dl of water in a heavy-bottomed pan (pot), covered, until the liquid has been absorbed, which should take around 7 minutes. Leave to swell and fluff up for a few more minutes.
- Set aside the cooked quinoa, which should still be slightly al dente, in a shallow dish, in one layer.
- Holding them with a fork, roast the whole aubergines over a flame for 1 minute on each side. Allow to cool for 10 minutes, then peel them and cut them into 2cm cubes.
- Dice the tomatoes, keeping the skin and seeds.
- Combine the ingredients in a large bowl when the quinoa and aubergine have cooled down (to room temperature). Mix thoroughly but quickly so as not to crush the diced tomatoes and aubergine cubes.
- Serve at room temperature, simply adding a few a cubes of ewes' milk Feta cheese. This salad (minus the Feta) can also be served as a side dish with grilled meat or fish.

Grilled vegetable salad with mozzarella di bufala

SERVES 4:

1 LARGE COURGETTE (ZUCCHINI), 1 MEDIUM AUBERGINE (EGGPLANT), 1 SWEET RED PEPPER, 2 HANDFULS ROCKET, 2 MOZZARELLA DI BUFALA BALLS, 125G EACH, EXTRA VIRGIN OLIVE OIL, 2 GARLIC CLOVES, CHOPPED, 1 BUNCH BASIL, SALT, PEPPER, 2 TOMATOES, CUT INTO LARGE CUBES, FRESH THYME.

FOR THE ACCOMPANIMENT: LEMON AND BALSAMIC VINEGAR.

To save time, use ready-prepared roasted vegetables, which can be found in most deli departments (fresh or canned). Choose a brand without preservatives. Carefully drain these vegetables, preserved in oil, by leaving them in a colander for 30 minutes.

- Cut the aubergine and courgette into thin (2-3mm) slices lengthwise. Preheat a clean cast-iron grill at maximum temperature for 10 minutes. Mark the slices of vegetable by criss-crossing them at an angle of 90° half-way through cooking. Allow 2 minutes for each side.
- Place in a large dish and season with salt, pepper, fresh thyme, olive oil and garlic.
- Holding it with a fork, roast the pepper over a flame for 1 minute on each side, so that it can be peeled. Marinate with the courgette and aubergine for 30 minutes.
- Season the rocket with salt, pepper and olive oil. Arrange the rocket on four plates and divide out the marinated vegetables equally.
- Slice each ball of mozzarella into 6 thin strips. Place on the vegetables and add the tomato cubes and the basil leaves.
- Serve accompanied by a lemon quarter and balsamic vinegar.

Green asparagus, raw ham and roasted pine nut salad

SERVES 4:

2 BUNCHES GREEN ASPARAGUS, 4 RIPE TOMATOES, 4 TBSP ROASTED PINE NUTS,

SALT, PEPPER, 4 TBSP EXTRA VIRGIN OLIVE OIL,

2 TBSP BALSAMIC VINEGAR, 4 SLICES RAW BAYONNE HAM, 1 BUNCH FRESH MIXED HERBS

(FLAT-LEAVED PARSLEY, BASIL, CHERVIL).

You can add 50g of Parmigiano Reggiano shavings.

Other varieties of raw ham can of course be used: Parma, Serrano or even organic Ardennes ham.

To roast the pine nuts, simply place them on a baking tray in a hot oven for a few minutes, turning and shaking it to ensure that the pine nuts do not burn on one side.

- Choose firm tomatoes and cut them into large cubes.
- If the asparagus is very thin, cut it half-way down, thus keeping only the spear. If the asparagus is normal to thick in size, peel the lower half with a potato peeler. Blanch in salted boiling water for 2-5 minutes, depending on the thickness. The asparagus should be al dente. To achieve this texture, refresh it with 2-3 litres of cold water (to which ice cubes can even be added) for 1-2 minutes.
- Drain and set aside in a colander.
- Put the asparagus and the cubes tomatoes into a large bowl. Season with salt, pepper, olive oil and balsamic vinegar. Arrange on four plates and put the slices of ham cut into four pieces around. Sprinkle with roasted pine nuts and herbs. Serve with toasted bread rubbed with garlic.

Sweet and sour vegetables and sardines

To turn this starter into a light yet complete dish, add halved hard-boiled eggs and a few cubes of just warm steamed potato cubes.

Choose simple, good quality sardines, not necessarily in olive oil. This rustic dish is very eye-catching and does not call for elaborate ingredients such as skinned, boned or spiced sardines and the like.
It is advisable to use sardines from a variety of countries, such as Portugal and Morocco. In France, some regions have restarted traditional cottage industry sardine canning, one example being the city of Quiberon in Brittany.

Did you know that canned sardines can be matured? Buy in a good stock and store them in a kitchen cupboard for at least six months, occasionally turning the cans over. The result is quite simply superb — and mouth-watering.

SERVES 4:

12 SARDINES IN OIL, 2 LARGE CUPS SWEET AND SOUR VEGETABLES, 2 LETTUCE HEARTS, 75ML (8 TBSP) OLIVE OIL. TO GARNISH: 1 LEMON, QUARTERED.

FOR THE SWEET AND SOUR VEGETABLES: 200G CARROTS, 200G CELERIAC, 200G TURNIPS, 150G FENNEL, 200G CAULIFLOWER, 2 LITRES BOILING WATER, 1 MEDIUM ONION, CUT INTO 12 QUARTERS (APPROXIMATELY 100G), 1 650G JAR (NET WEIGHT UNDRAINED) CRUNCHY SMALL PICKLED GHERKINS.

FOR THE FLAVOURED LIQUID: 1 SPRIG THYME, 1 BAY LEAF, 1 GARLIC CLOVE, 75G SUGAR, FRUCTOSE OR HONEY, 15 BLACK PEPPERCORNS, 1 TBSP CORIANDER SEEDS, 1 CLOVE, 6 JUNIPER BERRIES, 1 TBSP PINK PEPPERCORNS (BAIES ROSES), 1 TBSP SALT, 50CL WATER.

- The previous day, peel the carrots and turnips. Trim the vegetables. Cut into strips (6-7cm long and 6-7mm wide). Blanch in boiling water for 30 seconds, then drain.
- Put the drained vegetables and the jar of pickled gherkins with their vinegar into a large bowl. Place all the flavoured liquid ingredients in a pan (pot) and bring to the boil. Pour the hot flavoured liquid over the vegetables. Refrigerate for a minimum of 24 hours.
- Remove the larger outer leaves of the lettuce, keeping only the tender white heart. Separate the leaves, wash and dry. Arrange the lettuce leaves on four large plates, distribute the (drained) sweet and sour vegetables on the salad.
- Open the cans of sardines and remove them carefully, without breaking them. Arrange 3 sardines on each plate, season with a dash of olive oil and garnish with lemon quarters.

M'hamsa salad with
sun-dried tomatoes and fresh mint

The Mahjoub family is very proud of this m'hamsa (pronounced 'hamsa'), a typically Tunisian variety of coarse-grained couscous. Produced entirely by hand, it is made from hard (durum) wheat semolina, salt and extra virgin olive oil. The secret of its unique taste, texture and flavour lies in natural slow drying. From the purely practical viewpoint, it is cooked like pasta.

In Tebourba, it forms part of a traditional dish. It is served hot, with small pieces of dried and smoked mutton. Seasoned, naturally, with home-made spices.

M'hamsa can be eaten like pasta with a main dish. But it also ideal in easy to prepare 'one-pot' meals, for the whole family.

This salad can be adapted and supplemented as the mood takes you, with tomatoes, parsley, coriander, olives, artichokes and so on.

SERVES 4-6:

500G TEBOURBA M'HAMSA, 7DL SPRING WATER, 10G SALT,
20 PIECES SUN-DRIED TOMATOES IN OIL, 20 LEAVES FRESH MINT, EXTRA VIRGIN OLIVE OIL.

- Bring the water and salt to the boil in a medium-sized pan. Sprinkle the m'hamsa into the boiling water. Using a wooden spoon, mix gently so that the grains are evenly distributed in the liquid.
- Cover and cook over a medium heat for 5 minutes. Check whether the semolina has absorbed all the liquid. If not, cook for another 1-2 minutes. Turn off the heat.
- Add 2-3 tablespoons of olive oil. Cover again.
- When the grains have absorbed the water and olive oil, transfer to a large serving dish. Leave to cool down or to become cold, according to taste.
- Finely slice the sun-dried tomatoes and chop the fresh mint into thin strips. Mix well and serve

Spaghetti with sardines and stale breadcrumbs

Traditionally made harissa can easily be substituted for the chilli pepper.

When serving pasta with oil-based sauces such as pesto or aglio & peperoncino, try to cook the pasta for a minute less than indicated on the packet. Take a further minute off cooking time for more liquid sauces, mainly cooked tomato-based.

Semi-whole wheat pasta has a stronger, more pronounced taste, evocative of ripe cereals, than that of pasta made from white flour.

If you consider dry bread and canned sardines to be 'frugal' ingredients, spoil your guests with a good wine. This dish is full of character and a vintage wine will complement it perfectly!

SERVES 4-6:

400G SEMI-WHOLE WHEAT SPAGHETTI (SIZE NO 5), 8 GARLIC CLOVES, PEELED AND QUARTERED, 2 CANS SARDINES IN OIL, 1 SPRIG THYME, 100G STALE BREAD, 1 BAY LEAF, 1 DRIED CHILLI PEPPER, CHOPPED, 1 CUP FLAT-LEAF PARSLEY, CHOPPED, 10CL EXTRA VIRGIN OLIVE OIL, SALT, PEPPER.

- Put the sardines with their oil, the garlic, the thyme, the bay leaf, the chilli pepper and the roughly crushed stale bread into a non-stick frying pan or a wok. Brown the mixture until it is dry over a high heat for 3-4 minutes, using a wooden spatula to crush the sardines. Continue cooking over a very low heat for 10 minutes, until the mixture is golden brown, dry and crispy.
- Cook the spaghetti for 7 minutes in 3 litres of slightly salted boiling water (8g of salt per litre of water).
- Drain the pasta and pour over the sardine mixture, adding the parsley and olive oil. Mix together gently over a low heat, using two forks. Adjust the seasoning, adding salt and pepper and more chilli pepper to taste.
- Arrange in four hot spaghetti plates or bowls. Serve without Parmesan.

Spaghetti with harissa and niçoise olive paste

SERVES 4-6:

400G SEMI-WHOLE WHEAT SPAGHETTI (SIZE NO 5), 8 GARLIC CLOVES, COARSELY CHOPPED, 2 TBSP TRADITIONALLY MADE HARISSA, 1 TBSP OLIVE PASTE, 10CL EXTRA VIRGIN OLIVE OIL, 1 BUNCH PARSLEY, 1 SPRIG THYME, A FEW FRESH OR HOME-DRIED OREGANO LEAVES, 2 TBSP SALT-CURED WILD CAPERS, 4 SUN-DRIED TOMATOES IN OIL, SALT.

TO SERVE: PARMIGIANO REGGIANO OR PECORINO.

Harissa comes from the Arabic word "lhares" (to crush). Tebourba harissa, a speciality of the Moulins Mahjoub company, is of medium strength, enhancing the range of flavours of the dried chill rather than its pungency. It owes its exceptional taste to light smoking of the chillies. A great product!

- Brown the garlic in half the olive oil for 30 seconds. Add the harissa, the olive paste, the thyme, the oregano, the crushed capers and the sun-dried tomatoes in a fine julienne.
- Cook the spaghetti for 7 minutes in 3 litres of slightly salted boiling water (8g of salt per litre of water).
- Drain the pasta and pour over the garlic and harissa mixture. Finish off by adding the parsley and the rest of the olive oil. Mix together and serve immediately.
- Serve grated Parmigiano reggiano or Pecorino separately.

Organic and Fair Trade

I have always been interested in organic food. When I was 18, I used to bake organic bread at home on Sundays to take with me to eat during the week when I was away at school in Namur. I have always liked wandering around health food stores and I try to buy organic products to eat at home.

Just as a woman cannot be 'half' pregnant, I could not imagine Le Pain Quotidien moving into organic food half-heartedly. Once you have taken this step, it must be applied to everything that you offer to consumers.

I really had what might be called an organic 'revelation' after the opening of the stores in Los Angeles. In California, organic food is part of a lifestyle and is often combined with vegetarianism. I have been told that a sixth of the population of California is vegetarian.

Professionally, things are more complex on the face of it. Sources of supply are never regular and organic food's reputation for being a lot more expensive often proves true, but only superficially.

The sheer power of this phenomenon in California and the fact that it was mainstream prompted me to go and look for organic products where they were to be found. It was almost six months before I was able to display organic bread in the bakeries.

First I analysed the mass and volumes that we procured. Our biggest input was obviously flour. Four tonnes a day were used between New York and Los Angeles, meaning that we had containers on ships permanently sailing across the Atlantic from Antwerp. Obtaining supplies of stone-ground (non-organic) flour in Europe was still a viable proposition when the dollar was a strong currency. But with an unfavourable exchange rate, importing flour was becoming increasingly expensive, especially as the cost of storage was also a big drain on our resources and ultimately on our profitability. It also happened that for one reason or another, a cargo was blocked by the FDA (Food and Drug Administration) for further analysis. That could take weeks to complete and we ran out of supplies in the meantime. So we had already used local suppliers.

American millers offered us very good quality wheat but none of them produced real stone-ground flour. Stone grinding produces flour which is far finer than that ground in metal cylinders. Bread made from stone-ground flour has the more pronounced taste of the whole cereal and is crunchier, because the bran and flour particles are atomized better.

The dual conversion, to American and organic flour, came about simultaneously, when I found an organic flour brand which agreed to change the way in which its product was made. It subcontracted milling to a flour mill in North Carolina which worked with stones.

For several months it was basically a question of trial and error. There was quite a lot of to-ing and fro-ing until we got the right grind, the one which gives our bread its character and its special texture. In the end, we obtained an organic flour which cost the same as the 'normal' flour imported from Belgium. To be honest, we were also able to achieve this objective because we were cutting our transport and storage costs at a stroke.

The first step had been taken. We could hardly backtrack. Going on about organic products and foods, about protecting groundwater, bird life, etc., is all very well. But you can't claim to be saving the planet with bread and jam, whilst at the same time continuing to pollute it with milk and coffee. So going organic was a question of all or nothing.

It's here that the figures start to become meaningful – and that a minimum degree of tenacity is needed to achieve one's objective. The first organic milk bought from our distributor cost 80% more than regular milk. Overnight, the annual milk bill, extrapolated to all the New York and Los Angeles stores, went up by $200,000 a year. That's a huge amount for a product that we don't actually sell in our 'grocery store' but is merely something that goes with the coffee served to customers. It's hardly the sort of decision that can be taken lightly.

At that stage, if you want to continue going organic and to keep your stockholders on side, you have to bring down purchase prices. And that means sourcing your raw materials yourself.

That's how I found myself flying first to Chicago, then on to Madison, Wisconsin. After a night in a hotel, I had a three and a half hour drive ahead of me to LaFarge, which, with a population of just 100 and located in deepest Wisconsin, I imagined would be a godforsaken place.

I had an appointment at One Organic Way with George Siemon, CEO and founder farmer of the Organic Valley cooperative. With almost 700 members in all parts of the country, this organic cooperative is the largest of its kind in the USA. All the farmers are stockholders, which in practice means that they are masters of their selling prices. This is less innocuous than appears at first sight. It is not necessarily common knowledge that in the USA, dairy products are quoted on the Chicago Stock Exchange. The price of butter determines the price of a litre of milk, which thus fluctuates from week to week. In winter, all it takes is for there to be a snowstorm and the price can rocket. For other reasons the price can crash, meaning that farmers sell at a loss. Organic Valley sets the price of milk once a year. When you meet them they offer you a firm contract, protecting the producer and his customer against stock market fluctuations.

That was the sound basis on which we held our discussions and that they agreed to supply Le Pain Quotidien in both New York and Los Angeles with milk and eggs. And the arrangement suited me as my partner was a cooperative which had introduced a form of fair trade, encouraging 'sustainable agriculture'.

I have pleasant memories of the day I spent in Wisconsin. The headquarters of this company, which turns over $300 million a year, are in wooden cabins, fitted with computers. The boss is a dairy farmer whose cattle graze in a pretty valley in Wisconsin. He is a really nice and open kind of guy. We broke off our talks at lunch time and a secretary cooked wild mushrooms in cream for us.

I can't remember whether I started searching for coffee before milk. But the American way of life makes them totally inseparable.

Initially, we had served Lavazza, because they had helped us out when the Madison Avenue bakery and store had first opened. Afterwards I thought it was of fundamental importance to reinforce everything Belgian. For instance, I served Spa brand spring water for a long time, until the different distributors in New York stopped importing it.

For coffee, we used the Belgian coffee roaster Jacqmotte.

Unfortunately, its taste was not geared to American consumption habits. Looking at people in the street, you would see them walking around with litre size coffees to go. One or two measures of coffee, even roasted Italian style, was not enough to give the required strength to such a large volume. Especially as tastes had fundamentally changed. Starbucks, a large-scale pioneer, had been the driving force behind the move away from the very weak 'dishwater' coffee previously drunk by millions of Americans to espresso coffee. Americans had developed a new palate, looking for dark roast-tasting coffee. We didn't go that far, because we sought to preserve the fruit of the coffee, in the European tradition.

I remember that when I asked our Belgian coffee roaster to produce beans which I judged roasted enough, he told me that I was going too far and that my vision of coffee was sacrilegious.

Instead of responding to my request, he tried to make me accept his vision (at the time) of what coffee should be. And it wasn't strong enough for my taste. He probably believed that he was demonstrating something to me. But without success.

A year or two later, my coffee, the one that my roaster had found too 'extreme', had become the norm, exactly what his customers expected him to supply. I draw a number of conclusions from this experience. Firstly, tastes change very quickly. Secondly, acceleration is all the quicker as there is a large engine driving change, Starbucks in the case in point. And thirdly, it's better to be a trend-setter and pioneer, rather than jumping on the bandwagon when it's almost too late to catch up.

The main thing was to find organic coffee. Astonishingly, if you put such a request to a conventional supplier, he will try and dissuade you. He will only get his act together when you tell him that it's organic or nothing.

In the end, we found an excellent partner in Antwerp, Belgium and opted for an organic Arabica hard bean coffee, offering us both a signature and continuity. The coffee comes from Villa Rica, a high altitude district in Peru where top quality beans are grown. Subsequently, we developed a range of organic teas with the same supplier.

I also worked on other products, such as dried fruit and nuts, jams and jellies and fruit and vegetables. We were also still having difficulty in obtaining regular supplies of some products, such as red berries.

Meat, mainly hams, came at a fairly late stage in our research. Because it wasn't easy. In the USA, hams from organically reared pigs could be found, but the processing was not great. I failed to detect the touch of the traditional pork butcher whose family had been in business for three generations.

In Europe, on the other hand, I made a marvellous find, a co-operative in the Ardennes region of southern Belgium which reminded me of Organic Valley.

They were pig breeders and sold fresh meat but also processed the pork into ham, slicing sausage and pâté. When I went to see them in the town of Malmédy, I found a modern company which made a gourmet product using old recipes obtained from a small pork butcher in a nearby village, all in high-tech production facilities, meeting all the latest health and safety standards.

The pigs reared were very well treated, so well treated in fact that they were less stressed, meaning that the meat was of better quality. The cooperative – called Porc Qualité Ardennes – was also involved in carrying out in-depth work on selection of breeds of pig whose meat is slightly fatty. This is important for the taste. I'm convinced that organic is better, or let's say at least as good as the best 'classic' products.

Le Pain Quotidien first went organic in California. There wasn't a lot of hype. Customers were informed on postcards showing a field of wheat. On the back the following slogan was printed: "Bringing you the best organic products, we support sustainable farming for future generations." And I firmly believe that it's true!

Over and above principles, money was still the sinews of war. My partners had given me a free hand. But that's not to say that they would have accepted a decline in profitability.

I had done a great deal of work to secure supplies, cutting out middlemen as far as possible. But the extra costs associated with this type of agriculture cannot be avoided. So we passed them on, giving us a minimum safety margin. In practice, consumers benefited from all the work we had put in to find the products. We brought them organic products for the price of 'traditional' ones.

By 'going organic', we attracted customers who had not previously come to Le Pain Quotidien. Our stores, which had been open for six or seven years by then, were doing very well but had reached a plateau, so to speak. Going organic boosted their sales by around 15%. Offering organic products truly added a new dimension to Le Pain Quotidien.

Banana and pineapple clafoutis

SERVES 6-8:

3 BANANAS, 1 400ML CAN COCOA MILK (UNSWEETENED), 1 340G CAN PINEAPPLE SLICES IN THEIR OWN JUICE (OR 250G FRESH PINEAPPLE, PEELED AND SLICED), 3 EGGS, 2-3 SLICES BREAD, 150G FRESH CREAM, 150G MILK, 200G SUGAR OR FRUCTOSE, PEEL OF 1/2 LIME, JUICE OF 1 LIME, 100G GRATED COCONUT, BUTTER, 2 TBSP RHUM VIEUX (AGED RUM) (OPTIONAL).

- Preheat the oven to 200°C.
- Lightly grease a gratin dish. Cut the slices of bread (crust removed) into 12mm sticks. Distribute them evenly on the bottom of the dish so that it is covered completely. Peel the bananas, cut them in half lengthwise and place on top of the sticks of bread.
- Arrange the quartered pineapple slices around the bananas.
- In a bowl, beat the eggs and sugar with a whisk until the sugar has melted. Add the coconut milk, the fresh cream, the milk and the lime peel and juice.
- Pour the mixture over the bananas and pineapple in the gratin dish. Dust with the grated coconut and bake at 200°C for 30 minutes.
- Serve slightly warm, pouring over "Rhum Vieux" according to taste.

This recipe can be made using only one type of fruit (either banana or pineapple). Low-sugar biscuits, such as "Petit Beurre", can be substituted for bread. Small individual gratin dishes can also be used instead of a large one.

Fig clafoutis

As the fig season is short, this recipe can be made with figs that you have thought to freeze during the season. Choose small blue or black figs which are not too watery. Freeze them flat on a plate and put them in an airtight bag once they are nice and hard. Vanilla can be substituted for lavender. Use a pod split lengthwise, scraping out the seeds with the tip of a small paring knife. Put both the pod and the seeds in the cream.

You can also flavour the cream with a pinch of ground cinnamon or, even better, with a cinnamon stick infused in the cream and left as a garnish in the dish when it goes into the oven.

SERVES 4-5:

375G FRESH CREAM, 70G HONEY, 2 LAVENDER SPRIGS (INFLORESCENCES), 4 EGG YOLKS, 10 PETIT BEURRE BISCUITS, 12-15 SMALL BLUE FIGS, BUTTER.

- Preheat the oven to 200°C.
- Break the biscuits into 5-6 pieces. Distribute them evenly on the bottom of a lightly greased gratin dish (or in 4 small individual dishes).
- Remove the small hard stalk from the figs and halve them. Place them on top of the crushed biscuit mix (skin side facing down) and bake at 200°C for 10 minutes. Meanwhile, boil the fresh cream with the lavender springs. Remove from the heat as soon as the mixture comes to the boil.
- Mix together the egg yolks and the honey with a small whisk in a large bowl. Pour a third of the hot cream on the mixture.. Dilute well and add the rest of the cream.
- Take the figs out of the oven and pour the hot cream on top of them.
- Return to the oven for 10 minutes, lowering the temperature to 110°C so that the cream cooks gently.
- Serve slightly warm or iced, depending on the season.

Barley and soya (soy) milk and roast apricots dessert

SERVES 4-6:

120G BARLEY FLAKES, 8DL SOYA (SOY) MILK,

1 VANILLA POD (OR NATURAL LIQUID EXTRACT), 175G FRUCTOSE, NEUTRAL OIL.

FOR THE GARNISH: 6-9 FRESH APRICOTS OR 12-18 CANNED APRICOT HALVES

(SUGAR-FREE). 2 TBSP FRUCTOSE, FRESH MINT.

- Split the vanilla pod lengthwise. Scrape out the seeds with the tip of a small paring knife. Put the pod and the seeds into a pan containing the soya milk and barley flakes.
- Bring to the boil and simmer very gently with the lid on for 10 minutes. Add half the fructose and cook for a further 2 minutes.
- Add the rest of the fructose and cook for a further 2 minutes. Divide out the mixture, in 4 or 6 small moulds, lightly greased to make turning out easier. Refrigerate for at least 4 hours.
- Turn out the desserts onto a large serving dish or individual serving plates.
- Heat up a non-stick frying pan and dust the bottom with the fructose. Immediately place the apricot halves side by side, skin side facing downwards, in the frying pan. Caramelize over a high heat for 2 minutes on each side, until they are nicely coloured.
- Place 3 apricot halves on each barley cake. Decorate with a fresh mint leaf and serve.

This recipe can be simplified by substituting apricot coulis for roasted apricots.
To do so, mix the fresh or canned apricots with a small amount of fructose and 1 or 2 tablespoons of water or lemon juice if necessary to liquefy the coulis.

Pain perdu (French toast) with honey and spices

SERVES 4:

4 SLICES SOURDOUGH WHEAT BREAD (300G), 3 WHOLE EGGS,

1/2 LITRE TEPID MILK, 2 PINCHES CINNAMON, 2 PINCHES CARDAMON, 2 PINCHES NUTMEG,

2 PINCHES DRIED CLOVE, 100G ALL FLOWER HONEY, 40G UNSALTED BUTTER.

TO SERVE: FRESH BUTTER, LIQUID HONEY.

- Mix the honey with a pinch of each spice. Cut the slices of bread into 3 rectangles.
- Beat the eggs and the tepid milk. Add a pinch of each spice and leave the slices of bread to soak in this mixture for 5 minutes.
- Heat up two large non-stick frying pans and melt 10g of butter in each.
- When the butter is hot and frothy, carefully place 6 rectangles of bread in each frying pan and fry over a high heat for 1 minute on each side.
- Add 10g of butter when the rectangles of French toast are turned over the first time. When they are golden on both sides, put half the honey on the visible surface of the rectangles.
- Turn over and fry over a very high heat to caramelize. Add half the honey to the second visible surface and turn over to caramelize, still over a very high heat. Serve the French toast hot, with fresh butter and liquid honey separately, acacia honey, for example

Granola parfait

The interesting thing about this breakfast dish is the contrast between the crunchiness of the granola, the velvety smoothness of the yogurt and the freshness of the fruit. Soya milk or bifidus yogurt can be substituted for regular yogurt.

Le Pain Quotidien brand granola is made from a mix of cereal flakes, dried fruits and honey, all of which are toasted in the oven to produce its deliciously crunchy consistency.

SERVES 4:

400G ORGANIC GRANOLA, LE PAIN QUOTIDIEN BRAND, 4 PLAIN YOGURTS (125G POTS), 240G RED BERRIES (STRAWBERRIES, RASPBERRIES, BLACKBERRIES, BLUEBERRIES, ETC., DEPENDING ON THE SEASON), FRESH MINT LEAVES.

- Take a large milkshake glass with a stem and put a teaspoon of yogurt at the bottom.
- Add a third of the granola. Then add 3 tablespoons of yogurt and a second third of the granola.
- Finish off with the remainder of both the yogurt and the granola.
- Decorate with plenty of fresh fruit, adding a mint leaf as the final touch.
- Eat immediately, before the granola goes soggy.

Granita of peaches in wine

SERVES 6-8:

750G WHITE OR YELLOW PEACHES, WASHED AND STONED (PITTED), 100G FRUCTOSE, JUICE OF ONE LEMON, 25CL WHITE WINE.

FOR THE GARNISH: 300G FRESH FRUIT IN SEASON, CUBED PEACHES, GOOSEBERRIES, BLACKCURRANTS, CHERRIES, 1 BUNCH FRESH MINT.

- Put the peaches, white wine, lemon juice and fructose into the food processor bowl. Blend for 1-2 minutes until the mixture is smooth and creamy. Pour into a square earthenware or glass dish and freeze for 6 hours.
- Put 4 ice cream dishes into the freezer at least 30 minutes before serving.
- Take the granita out of the freezer and scrape it with a tablespoon, starting at a corner, to produce frozen fruit flakes. Half-fill the well chilled dishes and add a little fresh fruit. Fill the dishes to the top with the granita.
- Decorate with fresh fruit, piled high, and a mint leaf. Serve immediately.

Index of recipes

Soups

Tartines

Alain, Louella and Ines Coumont divide their time between a small farm-vineyard and bakery school located in the Languedoc-Roussillon region in southern France and the bread ovens of Brussels, Paris, New York, London, Beirut, Kuwait City, etc.

A pioneer and disciple of fair trade, organic agriculture and of gastronomy that is simple and respects traditions and cultures, Alain Coumont's avowed aim is to bridge the gap between the reality of the market economy and the new convivial humanism of an ecologically responsible twenty-first century.